HOW
THE RICH GET
DIVORCED

HOW
THE RICH GET
DIVORCED
(AND STAY RICH)

RYAN BENSEN

How the Rich Get Divorced copyright © 2025 by Ryan Bensen

Stay Rich Divorce Inc.
800 N King Street
Suite 304, #2233
Wilmington, Delaware 19801
www.stayrichdivorce.com

Publisher's Cataloging-in-Publication

Names: Bensen, Ryan, author.
Title: How the rich get divorced (and stay rich) / Ryan Bensen.
Description: Wilmington, DE : Stay Rich Divorce Inc., [2025]
Identifiers: ISBN: 9798998902017 (hardcover) | 9798998902000 (softcover) | 9798998902031 (ebook) |9798998902024 (audiobook)
Subjects: LCSH: Divorce--Economic aspects--United States. | Marriage settlements--United States. | Divorce--Law and legislation--United States. | Rich people--Family relationships--United States.
Classification: LCC: HQ834 .B46 2025 | DDC: 306.890973--dc23

To the husbands and wives who've been through hell—and made it out alive.

Contents

Tell Me What You Think

Let other readers know what you thought of *How the Rich Get Divorced*. Please write an honest review for this book on your favorite online bookshop.

★★★★★

What's Next?

So, what can you do? Besides taking to heart and to action the dolphin strategy of this chapter, you can join a network of others on the same journey and at the same stage.

Like the man jumping into that younger pool, I'm going to get a little bit naked with you: This is an upsell. I've created a private online community for men of means (proof of income and net worth required) who are currently in marital crisis—and for those who have just come out. It's all win-wins from here, in here, and we will teach you how to create them.

So get in here, if that's what you truly want but aren't sure how to make it happen—we'll make you sure either way and help you get and stay rich in the process, whether married or divorced.

Go to www.stayrichdivorce.com/forum to apply.

CHAPTER 1

DIVORCE WHEN THERE'S EVERYTHING TO LOSE

T here are three types of couples who divorce. Here they are.

1. Nothing to lose.

Because they have nothing. The first type of couple who divorces has nothing to lose because they have nothing. How would we recognize this couple? Stereotypically, they are lower to mid-income, maybe renting an apartment or have just bought a home. They are typically younger or just broke and may or may not have kids. Spousal incomes are usually fairly similar. The husband might work as a mechanic making $45,000 a year, and the wife works as an administrative assistant making $39,000. There's not much to fight over, and there are few assets, so divorce pretty much splits everything right down the middle, each getting 50 percent of the (limited) marital assets.

2. Nothing to lose but house and retirement.

The second type of divorcing couple is middle to upper class. They may be in W2 territory (the United States tax filing designation associated with a salaried position), or maybe one of spouses is a small business owner while the other is the W2. To be stereotypical (which we will be doing a lot of in this book, both for efficiency and for accuracy), the W2 wife might be a remote medical coder while her husband owns a very small family dental clinic. They have a pretty nice house in an OK suburb of a midsize city. Other couples in this category you might find (or already know personally) could include a union member and automobile industry worker husband and high school teacher wife. After twenty-five-plus years together, they have a reasonably nice home with around $400,000 to $500,000 in equity and some retirement savings like a pension plan.

In this divorce, there's more to lose—and more to be won, by one party. Usually, the dividing line here is this: We have two people both making middle incomes. The problem with this arises when neither party can front the cash to the other to make the equalization work for the division of family property, i.e., buying the other spouse out of the marriage since marital assets are jointly owned or managed. So most often, the wife keeps the house and the kids and the savings and the cars—and gets maintenance or alimony, plus child support—while the ex-husband has to restart his life at zero, which in his case means he's twenty-two years old again.

But less hair and lots of debt.

3. Everything to lose.

This divorcing couple type involves a high-income, high net worth husband and a part-time working or stay-at-home wife (who is also technically considered high net worth, thanks entirely to her husband). They married in their mid-twenties when their lives looked more like the first type of couple, but things took off. He earns seven figures a year, and his business success puts his company at an estimated $50 million valuation. They have investments, real estate, and expensive toys. And when they divorce, everything gets split down the middle, meaning *he* owes *her* $25 million, or half the business valuation. But where does that money come from?

What goes into the obvious (and incorrect) answer to that question is the same advice that's offered to the first two types of divorcing couples: Just split everything down the middle. Which translates to, *If there are assets, sell them.* For that second category of divorcee, often their marital estate division involves selling off the family home if the kids are grown (or there are no kids at all). Or if the home is retained, some other manner of divvying up occurs to make it "fair" from the court's perspective.

Now, map that category-two advice onto category three. Sell a privately held company, or write a $25 million check. Those are the two available answers. Both are unworkable to such an extent, they are laughable if not insulting. This "sell it or split it" advice, while ubiquitous for married couples considering divorce, completely miscalculates the financial situation, interests, and little-known available options for the high net worth (or "HNW," and refers to fortunes above $20 million) and ultra high net worth (or "UHNW," and refers to fortunes above $100 million). Yet advice offered to divorcees in this class is almost entirely nonexistent, at least in terms of its public availability. You have to "know a guy" if you're a high net worth individual in the midst of divorce and want not to lose all or most of it to legal fees, a vindictive ex, or both. Usually both. A book that tells all on this matter—and how to avoid it—does not exist. Until now.

"Get the Money. You Deserve It."

Most people's exposure to HNW and UHNW divorces is from tabloids, TV, or TikTok. Wherever they get their news, information, and entertainment—it's of course hearsay, just gossip, even if you are trying to learn something pertinent to your own situation or to that of a client's. It all amounts to non-advice, of course, which is a problem when action *is* required on matters of marital law and divorce proceedings because we default to what we know. For legal counsel, this means applying the first two categories' answers to questions of the third. That's how those HNW and UHNW divorces made headlines in the first place. Somebody got sloppy, somebody got greedy, or at least that's how it's reported, and it's all blown up in total public view. Not ideal from a public relations or personal branding perspective. And yet fighting it out in this way is the only path available when following the sell-it-or-split-it way. The divorcing parties' friends sometimes get their fifteen minutes of fame by contributing to the chaos, too, offering bad advice that compounds upon bad advice. *Get him. Show her who's boss. Screw her. Get the money. You deserve it.*

Those entrusted with providing legal counsel to such couples, while more educated, typically offer their HNW and UHNW clients advice that is no better than the couple's old college roommates feeding them terrible ideas to make everything worse. It's divorce porn.

This explains why I do what I do and with whom I do it. You see, much of my time is spent teaching lawyers how money works; most family lawyers don't understand how to read a financial statement, let alone figure out twenty in a complicated situation in which a husband's privately held business is valued at $50 million and the wife demands her half. What to do?

How to Get Divorce-Raped

In delicate divorce situations when everything is at stake for both parties, it seems like the only resolution is for one party to win big and the other party to lose bigger. In most marriages-turned-divorces, that's the wife "getting her husband's money" and the husband "losing everything." For example, the wife got $25 million but the husband was forced to sell his life's work before he was ready, and he also has to pay alimony and child support on top of that; in order to maintain his wife's lifestyle prior to divorce, he's going to be paying hundreds of thousands of dollars per month, spending down his $25 million in a few years until he is left with nothing, less than nothing (debt), and having to move back in with his parents and borrow Mom's car. His wife got literally everything, which she now gets to share with a younger male lover more fit and more attractive than the husband (again, I'll be continuing to use stereotypes throughout the book because, again, they tend to be accurate and therefore useful for both describing and predicting).

Such is the horror story we hear about in popular culture (or dream scenario, from the ex-wife's perspective). And yet this is not an exaggeration. It is the default outcome of the sell-it-or-split-it divorce advice provided by the mainstream.

Let me give you a slightly more realistic example. Not one from a high-profile divorce case that is rare but notable but rather a more common scenario—more common than you might imagine—but involves private individuals with a private business that's seemingly up for grabs amid divorce.

Capsizing the Love Canoe

Meet Bill and Sheri. Bill and Sheri met in university and got married after completing their degrees. Bill was a passionate entrepreneur who was into the outdoors and decided one day to start building canoes for their children when they were born. He thought they would build a canoe for them to go camping together.

In the meantime, what did they do for careers? Let's say that at the start, because it's typical, the wife was working in some sort of job while the husband pursued his passion. So Bill became a carpenter because he loved working with wood, and Sheri was a nurse.

When they had kids, Bill got into building canoes because he loved camping with his parents and thought this would be a great thing to do with their children. When people saw the canoe, they asked where they could buy one, but they couldn't because he had built just one. That spurred his idea to start manufacturing these canoes and selling them online.

Fast forward a few years and the canoe company became more successful, taking up a lot of Bill's time. Sheri could no longer stay employed because Bill was so busy, so she happily became a stay-at-home mom by choice to take care of the kids and take them to school, etc. This became more and more stressful as the canoe company grew and was distributing canoes in bulk across North America. Over time, Bill was spending all his time in the office as the CEO of the company, and Sheri would put the kids to bed and be left alone to herself.

Sheri got resentful, they grew apart; she built a friendship with their son's baseball coach, and one thing led to another. Sheri finally told Bill she "couldn't do this anymore" (which is what they always say once the guilt becomes too much, with that guilt being reassigned to the non-cheating spouse).

For the sake of brevity, we'll pass over the ensuing emotional turmoil and bitter accusations and disbelief and denial and so on, moving right into the financial question: What do they do? What happens to Bill's canoe business?

That great fifty-fifty split is the next step. But they can each get their own valuation for the business, which will be presented before the judge during trial (no, mediation did not work for poor Bill and Sheri). Sheri presents a valuation of $20 million. But Bill presents an independent valuation saying $6 million. Whatever the decided number, Sheri gets half; this is the default legal solution already baked in before any evidence for either case is presented. The judge compares the numbers, puts it in the middle because that's what judges do, and says $13 million. In reality, Bill can actually sell the company for $7 million, which he has to do now. Post-divorce, he owes Sheri a total of $13 million of which he's only paid $7 million (in order to account for the other assets the couple had jointly owned, all divided equally as well). The business is sold for the only price it ever could ($7 million), and Sheri is angrily waiting for her remaining $6 million payment to make up that $13 million total she believes she's owed. She thinks Bill must be hiding the rest somewhere.

This situation is the result of, among other things, the judge thinking both valuations were credible, and the lawyers not knowing how to articulate the financials. But really, it was the likeliest outcome for HNW and UHNW individuals when nobody advising either party knows how money works.

A Different Path

How do you prevent that from happening to you, in your situation, if you are divorcing? How do you prevent that from happening to your client, to the best of your ability and to the extent you can help as legal counsel, a financial planner, and so on?

Is there a **third way** besides bitter sell-it-or-split-it fights that make one party—the wealthier one—lose the divorce? Is there an alternative to getting sucked dry and moving back in with Mom? We know there is, as popular culture also reminds us that such-and-such superstar entrepreneur worth nine or ten figures has been divorced multiple times. Yet they did not start over from less than $0 each time. What's the difference? I know it because I've seen it.

Keeping the Rich, Rich, through Divorce

This is what I do. I'm pretty good at it. Let me explain.

- For more than ten years, I have worked on HNW and UHNW cases, mostly with women, and have seen the tricks men try. I have worked as an expert or consultant running litigation strategy on behalf of the woman's attorney (Attorneys tend not to understand the big driver of the HNW and UHNW cases. Hint: It is always the money.)
- My expertise crosses several professional designations in accounting, business valuations, financial forensics, and fraud examination, as well as an MBA.
- I have almost the whole alphabet behind my name, which is ironic for a supposed "numbers guy." These include Master of Business Administration (MBA), Certified Public Accountant (CPA) This is Chartered Professional Accountant, Chartered Accountant (CA), Chartered Business Valuator (CBV), Accredited in Business Valuation (ABV), Certified Fraud Examiner (CFE), and Certified in Financial Forensics (CFF).
- I have been engaged more than 1,000 times as an independent and unbiased expert at divorce trials.
- I have also been hired as a secret consultant to quarterback the entire litigation strategy behind HNW and UHNW cases for the

majority of attorneys who are inexperienced and untrained in the specific nuances of money, wealth, and power.

- I have personally uncovered over $100 million in hidden assets scattershot across the world.
- I have witnessed all the stories: mafia, "hookers and blow," international money laundering, gold, vaults of cash, crypto millionaires, swingers, "lost" watch collections, secret cam girls, affairs of one spouse, affairs of both spouses, family secrets, and every other skeleton in the closet.
- I have contributed towards successful men going bankrupt and into despair (my client was their ex-wife).
- I have also helped successful men walk away unscathed with a happy and financially stable ex-wife, children, and their business thriving.
- I am a hero to clients and a villain to their exes, but since you're reading this book, I am the author of your success.
- I have worked on more than 1,000 cases with clients across North America and Europe. I have also worked with men in assisting them with this process, through trial, and among a gambit of options.

I offer this special class of the world's wealthiest people what they need before they need it. The results are staggering. For example, one recent client's wife had cheated on him before they broke things off. He'd received a phone call from his neighbor's wife one day, saying, "Please tell your wife to stop fucking my husband." There was then a contentious battle over his assets ($150 million), but my client paid $0 in the divorce. He kept it all—because of the strategies you'll learn in this book. There are many more cases just like this across all levels of wealth.

Now, why hasn't this book already been written, and by someone like me? Again, because family lawyers know nothing about financial issues, and they tend to rely heavily on people with financial training in these cases. I built my practice with "bigger fish," meaning the very high to ultra high net worth individuals—it's a specialization within a specialization. I deal with clients only worth more than $10 million, generally $30 to $100 million-plus. There isn't a lawyer out there who does these files full time. They are few and far between, spread across North America. An attorney is licensed to practice in one or two states. Lawyers tend to have W2 files, with perhaps four complex matrimonial litigation files over the course of two to three years. And they consult with third party experts to run those files for them (like me).

Strategic elements are not allowed to be discussed by lawyers within the confines of the client-attorney relationship. That's the vast majority of what's in this book, like managing earnings and partner expectations in advance of divorce. Professional standards prohibit this. I am not confined to their taboo. I don't represent an individual in court or a divorce case. My profession is forensic accounting. Our job is to know the taboo. Someone has to. That's me.

So then why hasn't a forensic accounting specialist done a book like this? Likely because most work inside large firms, get busy, and focus on their local jurisdiction. They handle 100 cases a year, charge $40,000 a pop, and stay happy with that.

I took a different path. Early in my career, I was invited to meetings and events where I made the acquaintance of various elements of the gray market. Those acquaintances turned friends and colleagues gave me my first tour into the world of the ultra high net worth. It was all trust agreements. You know those guys who can drive fifteen Lamborghinis and have 600 properties but are broke on paper? That's what I witnessed firsthand for the first time. And it was all, strictly speaking, *legal*. This is precisely why I'm brought in early into the client-attorney relationship, to answer the difficult questions and set expectations among this class of earners and asset owners, usually to talk women "down" and men "up." Soon you'll learn what I mean by that and why it may be the most important takeaway from this book. Until we get there, here's how I'd like you to read it.

How to Read This Book

Take notes as you read. This is "how to get divorced and stay rich"; not how they *did* it with emphasis on specific example analysis, but how they *do* it. Think common patterns past and present, from even *years* prior to the divorce—which is when the HNW and UHNW begin thinking about this, long before most all other couples of other socioeconomic strata do.

And if you have any questions come up as you read, send them directly to me. Learn more about my firm and contact us at www.stay-richdivorce.com.

CHAPTER 2

💰

BEFORE THE RICH DIVORCE, THEY DO *THIS*

I want to be clear about who "the rich" refers to. "The rich" are those who **became** rich, not the already high net worth whose wealth came from family money or pre-marriage success. For that class, divorce is easy and boring. It goes like this:

- Get a prenup.
- Have family trusts.
- Get a postnup.
- Separate.
- Hire attorneys to bicker over clauses.
- Settle and pay some money.
- Let the judge approve.
- Divorce.

Boring. This book is for those who made it, usually men, and for those who advise or otherwise work with them. This is for those who "made it" while married and are now thinking, *Oh, shit.* Their stories typically go like this:

The couple got married at twenty-five. The man graduated from university, began his career, and started a side business; she has a job. They met in college. Not long after, his business takes off, and over the next ten years, a couple of kids come along. The woman quit her full-time job after kid one and her part-time job after kid two. The math didn't make sense given how much income her husband's explosive-growth business brought the family. And yet he's not home anymore, she stays home and doesn't get out, and both are miserable with the *status quo*. They never planned for this. When they got married, there was no expectation this man would be worth $50 million—or his wife by extension, as they have always been "married filing jointly," as their US-based tax return says. So how would the hyper-successful entrepreneur man have possibly taken preventative measures to protect himself if something were to happen? Affairs could happen, whether it's him straying into opportunistic temptation, her cheating out of spite or loneliness, or both at the same time. Or, addiction could strike—again, his, hers, or both. Or, they could lose money followed by a massive lifestyle downgrade, with promises that he'll rebuild one day (promises that she doesn't believe). Or, the husband, formerly in the back seat of a female-led relationship, matures into a confident, masculine man, and his feminist wife does not want to give up "wearing the pants." Her ego is unable to handle the new dynamic where she is no longer able to successfully boss her husband around; he speaks up for himself, telling her "no" when appropriate, and that is just about the end of the world for her.

Whatever the cause, it's now clear: This thing is over. If the wife files for divorce, it's two years after she decided it's over. Generally speaking, that's what to expect—she wants to be 200 percent sure and so gives her husband every chance she can to change (or in some cases, to change back). He's usually unaware of her agenda. But if the husband files first, it's likely after an argument as a snap decision and follows one or two phone calls to a buddy's lawyer.

If he follows the typical advice, he's going to lose big. He's going to lose half his net worth, minimum. And he has no idea.

How the Rich Think (and Divorce) Differently

The non-rich who marry, get rich, divorce, then stay rich treat their marriage differently than the typical couple who splits everything evenly or is forced to split that primarily husband-earned wealth right down the middle (usually husband-earned but this scenario has occasionally befallen female entrepreneurs, investors, and founders). The rich who divorce and keep the vast majority of the business, investments, assets, and cash they've worked so hard to acquire during the marriage think of their marriage in this way, and certain behaviors naturally follow:

The rich are always prepared to get divorced.

And so they run their business and manage their finances with that outcome in mind as a real, actual possibility. Because the less they prepare, the more they stand to lose to their ex in divorce. This preparation is done years in advance, usually after the first $3 to $5 million in net worth. Here's why.

In every divorce case, the judge reviews financial records from the past three years, often as far back as five years. Ergo, that's how far in advance the primary earning party, usually the husband, must prepare for divorce. Because everything is considered. Everything is scrutinized. It's all fair game. The divorce-unprepared, when that sudden filing comes, panic. There is a "divorce dive" in the business earnings that casts great suspicion and looks intentional. Other account balances plummet. There are numerous transactions to previously unused vendors, all in attempts to hide cash and offload assets. And it's all a noose the wealthy individual is using to hang their case metaphorically. It's *obvious* there's something to hide, and the (terrible) effort to hide it persuades the court to look for it (and find it).

Does this mean the high net worth couple in which divorce is a possibility for financial reasons are looking for an out from their marriage at any given moment? Certainly not. Even in happy marriages, preparation for the worst-case scenario is good business sense. "Fences make good neighbors," the saying goes. The rich consider: What are the consequences of leaving? And how might they mitigate those consequences, if at all possible? The rich have an open-door marriage (not an open marriage); they make it OK for the other spouse to leave. This is the proper perspective. *You take your business; I take mine. You can have the house; I'll take care of the kids. OK?* There's a healthy emotional detachment, which keeps the couple on their best behavior with one another. They don't butt heads because they're not stuck in a house together like some kind of prison. They are free. There are options. Usually the man has more hypothetically than the woman does. Consider a multi-multi-millionaire fresh out of a marriage versus a forty-five-year-old single mom of two—who is going to have the best "options"? This unspoken realization motivates the wife to respect her husband and allow behaviors she might otherwise not—including casual flings with other women (yes, I'm serious). All things considered, she has much to be grateful for in the marriage, much she would lose should she divorce her husband over his casual encounters with women.

This is the perspective of those who divorce and stay rich have, either upon entering the marriage or from having developed it over time. It is politically incorrect to discuss and yet entirely correct. Bottom line of these inconvenient truths: The married rich never feel like they or their partner has to stay. And that abundance frame goes a long way to ensuring both parties *want* to stay—and *not* want to leave. Both are critical to the success of the marriage, if it is to last.

So then, how *specifically* do the rich prepare to be divorced? What *specifically* does it mean to always be ready?

Let's Teach Divorce Accounting 101

The objective of divorce preparation in advance is straightforward, and it begins with a singular objective on the part of the breadwinner in the family: *I don't want to earn or own as much on paper.*

Being the responsible party, the high(er) net worth individual (in the marriage) should recognize that they're the person who's going to be left holding the bag. And it's going to be empty (or mostly empty) In other words, they're the payor versus the payee.

Basically, the way that divorce accounting works for this class is as follows: Let's say a guy has one or two businesses (to make it simple), and his wife makes marginal income from something part-time while raising the kids. When they entered the marriage, both were at zero in terms of assets, much less net worth. They went through college and were both at zero, then a few years into this marriage, his business took off. He's making a bunch of money, and she's making . . . whatever she makes. The question then, if they divorce, effectively becomes: **How much does this guy make, and what is the value of everything that they own versus whatever the liabilities might be?** Think mortgage, business loans, and so on.

How this gets complex with self-employed individuals specifically is that there are variations in income based on market trends or the trajectory of the business. There are also planned variations in income for tax purposes, where they're trying to minimize taxes, among other goals.

The entire framework that the legal system works with when assessing income for alimony or child support is taking somebody who's self-employed, has a bunch of tax benefits, and has other benefits tacked on, and saying, "How much money would this person need to make if they were just a W2 employee to afford their lifestyle?" It's a way of backing into W2 employee income when obviously they're not W2 employees, and there's a planning element installed. The question is why adjustments are being made, which is where looking at the last three to five years becomes more relevant.

In many cases, the court will look at a person's business income over the past few years and take an average. For example, let's say Geoff's mechanic business grossed $75,000, then $100,000, and then $125,000 in the last three years; the court might say his income is really around $100,000.

Secondarily, when it comes to the division of assets, let's say there's a house worth a million dollars, cars, and other items worth $500,000 net without any liabilities. That's $1.5 million. Then the question becomes, how much is Geoff's business worth? Because that's the last outstanding piece of the puzzle that needs to be argued over. That result is generally going to drive all the other decisions in the equalization of assets, because it's almost always the driver in higher net worth cases.

If there's $1.5 million in assets and then a $15 million business (in valuation), the total is $16.5 million, which means that $16.5 is to be split right down the middle. Except that valuation can be a gray area, as we've already discussed.

Another point to consider in the division of assets: Most jurisdictions are no-fault, meaning fault doesn't impact the equalization of assets. But in certain jurisdictions, the high net worth individual can apply for an at-fault judgment. This can help. But it doesn't necessarily mean that if it was going to be a fifty-fifty split, it will now be thirty-seventy because, for example, the other spouse cheated. No-fault divorce laws were introduced partly because in the past, husbands were often quite abusive, and wives were stuck in relationships because they had to prove fault to leave. Now, a spouse can leave for any reason and it very likely won't impact the financial settlement at all, although there's always a reason that gets discussed. If a spouse was abusive and caused the other to be psychologically impaired from future employment, the impaired spouse could potentially go after additional tort damages, similar to a motor vehicle accident or slip and fall case.

Judges have become more sophisticated and specialized in family law and are aware of the games people play to avoid a high income assessment or an overwhelmingly high business valuation. Judges can impute income if a person's claimed income doesn't match their lifestyle. For example, if a high net worth individual claims their business makes no money but they drive a new Porsche, wear a Rolex, and live in a 4,000 square foot house, the judge can determine that their income is clearly not zero.

To determine imputed income, judges can look at a high net worth individual's lifestyle and spending, such as bank and credit card statements, and calculate how much pre-tax income would be needed to support that. Judges can also look at changes in net worth over time. For example, if a person was worth $500,000 one year and $1 million the next year according to their taxes, but only declared $100,000 in income, the court may question where the other $400,000 came from and whether income was actually much higher than declared.

That being the background—and how an accounting of the couple's personal finances are done in divorce—how do the rich avoid that default state of an even split of everything? How does the partner with more to lose make it disappear on paper?

Divorce Accounting, Graduate School Edition

There is a certain level of sophistication to owning nothing on paper, paying little to no tax (which is another reason the rich tax these divorce prep measures), and yet being able to access resources any time anywhere. Their personal financial situation looks like this—first the business, then them personally. Visual aids support:

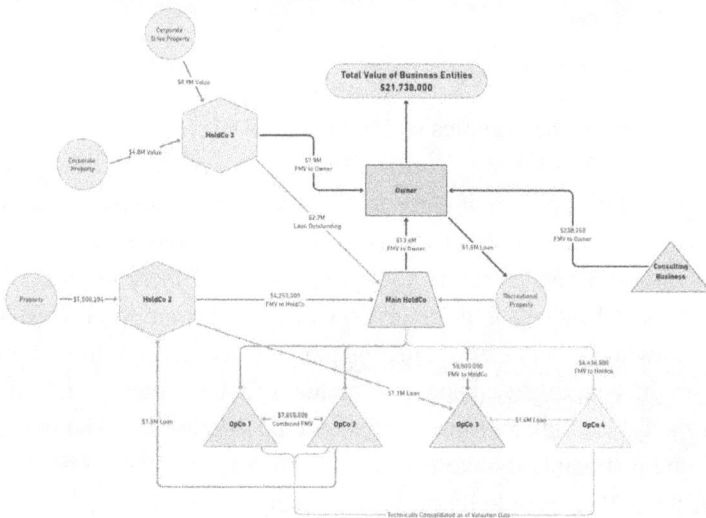

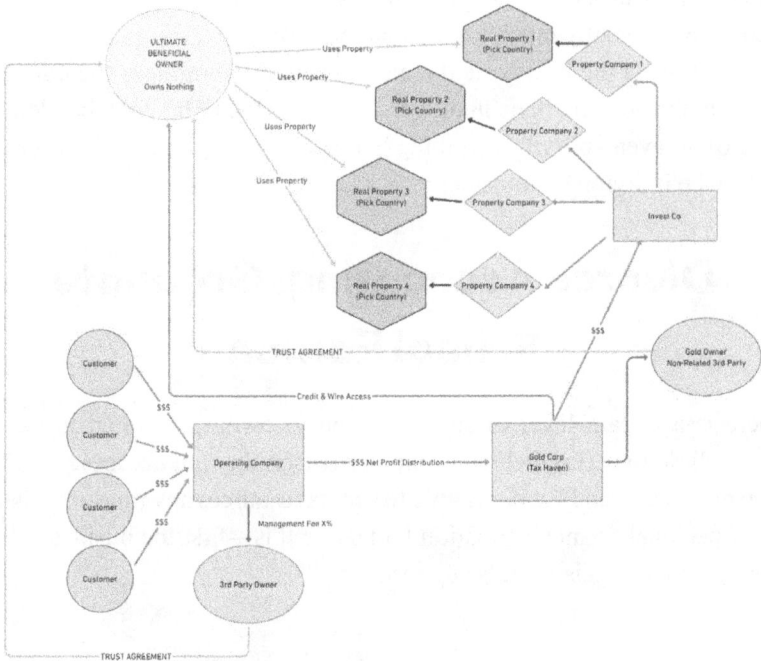

Let's unpack the graphics so it all makes sense.

The best way to wedge yourself into a lower settlement in a divorce case is to put up significant barriers to entry to get personal and business financial information compiled. In that respect, the more confusing it is, or the more moving pieces there are, the better. If there are a bunch of companies and money is going everywhere, and some things are being disclosed while others aren't, creating a big messy web, the more you can drive up the cost to get an accurate picture of what's going on. The wife (most likely) will take a lower settlement amount because she gets frustrated and just wants to take the bare minimum. At a certain point, after five years of this, people just say in as many words, "I'm done . . . just give me something." That's a strong play.

To review and extend: How it works as a setup over time is that the husband has a business that starts generating significant income, as I said, to the extent that there's a lot of disposable income. The first step is for

people to figure out how much money they need to take down personally to pay for everything. How much money do they need personally
versus how much can they just keep in the corporation to avoid paying
personal tax when drawing it down? That's tax arbitrage number one.
Then they might give the wife a salary of $100,000 too, so they can split
the income that way.

Next, they might set up a holding company to buy the building where
the business operates from so they can start stripping the profit from the
operating company to the holding company. That money will pay for the
real estate investment. Once that's taken care of and assuming everything
just keeps skyrocketing, it becomes a question of what to do with all the
excess money that's being collected because they don't necessarily need
it. They have to do something with it, otherwise it's just sitting in the bank
account losing its purchasing power due to inflation.

At that point, the rich start thinking about how to reduce the profit of
the operating company, which is going to take the biggest hit in divorce.
How do they reduce profit, mitigate adverse tax consequences, and start
investing this money into other stuff to make it grow over time? Tradi-
tionally, people who do this will set up a holding company for real estate.
Then they might set up a holding company or trust for the business interest to take away the corporate liability with litigation and shield it under
a trust agreement for the betterment of the kids.

Once it hits a certain point, they might start investing in stocks,
cryptocurrency, and other financial instruments. They might buy another
business, start merging with other businesses, or set up a second or third
business. For example, a rich small business entrepreneur might have a
trucking company along with the property, then invest in a mechanic's
shop that needs an equity investor, then set up a holding company for that
business. They might start up a tire distribution company to import Pirelli
tires. It all starts building in scale, and there's money going between all
these different businesses as loans, expenses, and revenue.

When it gets to a certain wealth level of $50 to $100 million and an
income level over $10 million, it becomes a question of how to keep all

the stuff they like and stay where they are, but pay no tax. That's what all this is building towards. Eventually, it becomes a question of how to profit-strip. Then it hits offshore businesses, and the question becomes how to start that profit-stripping but still have access to the money on demand. That's when offshore consulting companies, financing, restructuring, or bankruptcy of the business come into play, where suddenly it's in somebody else's name but they still own it—without owning it. They have access to everything to do with it and control it but don't own it on paper; all the money goes to a foreign country.

At that point, it becomes a question of how to get the money back if needed, or how to have access to the lifestyle that comes with the money. Shell corporations and holding companies are set up to own property, and credit cards and wire transfers are used to pay the bills.

The way this all works is that the rich individual's company in, for example, Indiana takes a loan or hires a consulting company based offshore somewhere, like the Cayman Islands. They start stripping and sending the profit from Indiana to the Caymans, but not in the person's name. The business in Indiana makes enough for the person and their family to live, paying for household expenses. But what if they want a second, third, or fourth house, or want to travel or invest? From the Cayman Islands, they set up different holding companies for international real estate. If the wealthy individual wants a house in Barcelona, the Cayman Islands company lends the money to the holding company for the house that's been bought in Barcelona. They can go to Barcelona whenever they want and go to their house, but they don't technically own it because it's owned by a holding company, which is held by someone else in trust. The person that owns the holding company is not them. For other expenses, they get an American Express Platinum card with a $100,000 spending limit, and it gets paid by the Cayman company. They can buy a bunch of stuff and don't have to worry about it.

Technically, the individual in question is supposed to provide all these records in their divorce, but often they conveniently forget, or the records are never kept in their home and so are not easily found. Nobody knows how it works, and that's the point. All the cars are owned by other people, the assets are owned by other people, the profit centers are owned by other people, and all of it filters into this web of different companies that pay the bills and allow for the desired lifestyle without any of it showing up as personal income.

From an uninformed perspective, this looks like tax fraud, but from an informed perspective, several expensive international tax lawyers are ensuring that it's 100 percent legal, or at least legal enough. There's a big cost to keeping this up, but it's still worth doing if there's $100 million or even $50 million at stake and the goal is to pay the wife $5 million instead of $25 million.

It creates a huge hurdle for the other side to try to get any of this information, and even then, the realistic probability of being able to actually pin the number in court is low. It becomes a settlement offer of $5 million now, or else the other side needs to try to subpoena or obtain records from six different countries and have ten people come and provide information, which is very difficult. The people in these offshore jurisdictions can just ignore the requests.

For most high net worth cases, it doesn't get to this level of financial sophistication necessarily because the numbers aren't as high. But it does usually still involve several companies, a holding company or some holding companies, and a real question mark on how much the assets or business assets are worth and how to calculate that.

High or ultra high net worth, the divorce becomes a question of where's the money and how it can be tied down to this person . . . *or not.*

So to bring it all back around . . .

Before the rich divorce, they ensure years in advance that they will stay rich. This happens as soon as they begin to get rich, at least for the smart ones who possess the abundance frame and see the mutual benefit in the open-door policy. In the case of the twenty-five-year-old, around age thirty, he begins making these key decisions for tax purposes, then for marital welfare purposes, move by move. So by age thirty-five to forty, the couple is successful, owns nothing on paper, owns everything practically, and is likely to have a far happier marriage and keep way more of their money (through *legal* tax avoidance strategies) than those who simply hope for the best.

Now, those who do (and those who don't) apply these strategies may think they are probably unnecessary if the marriage seems to be in healthy shape. But is it?

CHAPTER 3

THE MARITAL AUDIT

For whatever reason, common marriage advice has been reduced to one-sentence quips that are often misleading and drive the exact opposite behavior from what could be successful, with "Happy wife, happy life" being the most common, leading high net worth men into a perverse form of indentured servitude to a wife who in the vast majority of cases does not work outside the home. This reverse polarity eventually reveals itself outside the home, with a formerly confident and perhaps cocky founder, entrepreneur, or investor shriveling up into a "nice guy" who second- and third-guesses every decision.

In the cases I have dealt with personally, the majority of husbands were blindsided by a divorce everyone else saw coming—even the man's employees. Those otherwise street-smart individuals had not thought to check in on their relationship status until their wife set it to "over."

Naturally, men struggle more with the divorce process as a result of their shock. Meanwhile, as I said, the wife has typically made the decision to leave years ago and has already processed the emotions of leaving prior to separation or filing, whichever comes first.

Writing this, my friends Joe and Andrea come to mind. I met them both years ago at a professional conference. Joe was a successful (and wealthy) entrepreneur, and Andrea had experienced some success in life prior to becoming a stay-at-home mother. By all accounts, this duo appeared to be a power couple going places.

In dealing with Joe over many years, I noticed a rigidity in his life that was difficult to place. At certain times, he would be free for dinner, but most of the time he would not be with no real explanation as to why.

I also noticed that Joe had a Cinderella-like fixation on the time. He would frequently glance at his smartwatch or his phone in increasingly close intervals until finally saying, "Oh, wow, it's nine o'clock already. Have to go," and exit quickly thereafter.

Andrea, on the other hand, seemed to lead a fairly non-rigid life and had gotten into fitness and nutrition once their kids reached elementary age. But over that same time, Joe looked more tired and lethargic. He had withdrawn from the image of success he once projected.

One day Joe called me and confided in me something that was obvious to everyone but Joe—his marriage was in a lot of trouble. He was lost and didn't know what to do.

I then walked Joe through the casual yet necessary marital audit every happily married HNW and UHNW couple completes (and passes) in their own way. No discussion of this class of married couple is complete without it.

Do the Audit, Take the Tests

How healthy is a marriage really? Most high net worth men don't know until it's too late to do anything to salvage the relationship. (Note: Some couples need nothing else to improve their relationship; all is and will be well. In fact, the rest of this book is not worth the time for them to read. But for other couples, for those who fail this audit, the rest of this book is relevant to their situation. Why? Because this couple is likely to get divorced unless significant changes are made.) We will perform this audit by running a number of tests. Here is the first one.

The Blowjob Test

This one is crass, yes, and necessary. *When was the last time you got one?* The wealthy man who doesn't remember—or worse, he does, and it was eight years and eight months ago—indicates ill health of the marriage. This test works because it's an indication of attraction, wife to husband and husband to wife but particularly wife to husband. If the answer to the question is not "this morning" or "two nights ago" or some similar answer, it is likely the case that the husband is no longer the man his wife fell in love with. She just doesn't respect him and it shows.

The Stranger Test

Most relationships have a brokenness to them over time. But newlyweds, with a spark and energy, receive boundless compliments. As the years go by, the praise fades. How rare is it to hear after six . . . seven . . . sixteen . . . . twenty-seven years, "Wow, you are such a great couple. How long have you been together?" Such praise from a stranger indicates the passing of this test. Just consider the last time you approached total strangers and gave them an unsolicited compliment. Now imagine how comfortable and inspired you'd have to be in someone's presence to let them know how the energy they're giving off feels.

The rubric for the test is that it must be a stranger, not a family member or friend. "You guys make a great couple." Thanks, Dad. Someone you've never met before passing you on the street (sober, of course) issuing a compliment to a couple about their obviously healthy dynamic counts. That is the right track.

Failure of this test is not getting such praise at all; it's hearing no third-party compliments for your relationship from strangers since you were just married. Most people's close relationships are dysfunctional, and yours is no different, so you don't stand out. Therefore, no praise. Not good. Fix.

The Photo Test

The Photo Test involves looking back at photos of the couple together and examining the body language. Are they close together or far apart? If it's a group photo, are the husband and wife standing beside each other or at opposite ends of the group? Look also for crossed arms and other obvious indications someone is uncomfortable, perhaps not smiling naturally. Does the photographed couple look like they just had a fight and hadn't kissed and made up yet—or probably won't?

Another iteration of the photo test is masculine-feminine polarity. Is the man leaning in towards his wife, and she away from him? Does she look "strong" and is he just simply "nice"? Take it further: Imagine the image were photoshopped and two versions created. In one, the husband is removed. Is the wife obviously missing someone or something she had been draped around or leaning on? Test, passed. But now the alternative: If the wife is removed from the photo of the couple, is the man solitary yet complete? Does he look confident, ready, set in his ways? This is good. But the inversion—a weak man and an independent woman—is a failure of the test. Anything other than a proper leader-supporter dynamic is failure. And anyone can tell from one look at a photo.

The Permission Test

"I am" versus "Can I?"—the way a high net worth man speaks to his wife about upcoming activities, trips, or anything else outside previously scheduled activities that pull him away from her is telling. This is a declaration of intent versus a request for permission. This is the test: Does the man treat his wife like his mother, acting like a little boy who needs approval or validation?

Failure of the test indicates the husband is afraid of his wife. A colleague several years ago abandoned a client trip outside the country last-minute and burned the relationship with that client—simply because he was afraid of how his wife would react when he told her he would be going on a business trip and wouldn't be able to bring her along.

A nice guy and his money are soon parted.

The Change of Plans Test

How does the high net worth wife respond to a sudden change of plans? For example, "Oh, we're not going here tonight; we're going there." What is the wife's openness to change? Her trust in the man's decision-making capability?

Now, this does not have to be (and should not be) abrasive. "I have an idea." "Let's go there." "We should do this instead." These all work. After all, it's a loving relationship.

There needs to be a justifiable reason, by the way. It shouldn't be something like, "I want to go hang out with my friends instead of spending our anniversary dinner together." If that's what the man considers a reasonable deployment of the test, he has already failed it.

That said, for a classic Change of Plans Test, failure is any negative feedback from the wife, from whining to responding with a flat-out "no."

The Lifestyle Change Test

Suddenly, the wife alters her lifestyle without explanation, going from, for example, being a homebody with the kids to drinking with her friends, from being in the kitchen and enjoying delicious meal prep to being at the gym three times a week for two hours and eating salad at every meal . . . alone. Think major unexplained shift. *That's weird*—anything like that is a failure. And it's done alone by the wife, away from her husband. New activities together are ideal, such as ballroom dancing lessons or a new destination trip once a month as a mini-honeymoon with outdoor adventures unlike any the couple has tried before. But a sudden change in which the wife focuses her attention away from her husband indicates test failure.

The Check-MATE Framework Test

MATE here stands for **money**, **attention**, **time**, and **energy**. These are the four currencies a man can spend in any of his relationships to invest in the success of it. Is the husband spending his currency wisely? The right investment strategy creates a balanced portfolio.

Reaching the right amount with each of them is key, contrasted with, for example, providing all money and little to no attention, time, or energy. Or giving attention and time, yes, but the wife can tell her husband's mind is elsewhere; he's distracted, on-edge, anxious. Or offering time, attention, and money, yes, but being a fuddy-duddy—sapping her energy with complaints.

Ironically, money is the least valuable reward to the woman. Because for HNW and UHNW men, their time, attention, and energy are very expensive. They're not getting it back, and they could be using that time to earn more money. Perhaps not ironic after all. But what *is* ironic is that money is usually his greatest concern and yet the least of hers. As the saying goes, "A Ford-150 in the driveway is worth more than a Lambo that's never there."

Consider the high net worth wife who cheats: A woman often falls for whoever is nearest to them—and usually whoever invests in her children, like the kid's sports coach. It's "fish in the barrel" for that guy even though he might be a semi-unemployed electrician who earns in a year what her husband earns each week. By Tuesday.

This is an inversion of "hypergamy," the tendency for women to prefer higher-status men over their current lower-status spouse. You've heard of being money-rich but time-poor. After wealth achievement, money on paper no longer impresses a woman. Now her attention shifts to the men in her inner circle who might be money-poor (or at least poorer) but time-rich. They are willing and able to give her what her husband will not. It's *time-pergamy*. Most women are not motivated by a man's money; it's used only as a proxy for initial choice, vetting, and filtration.

By the way, this explains divorced female psychology—why women can be vindictive or perceived as such. This is because she feels she's been the victim of a long fraud. The illusion of what she thought her life would be is over and gone. Her husband seemed to offer her all his attention, time, and energy, then substituted it all for money once the latter became available in great supply.

To pass the Check-MATE test, the husband should spend more time, attention, and energy on his wife than he does money. Easy said, hard done.

Failing the Audit, Then Fixing It

The HNW or UHNW couple who fail one or more tests is not at a loss. Healing is possible. The way out is through. What is that way? Leadership command, in short.

The root problem is that the husband stopped leading at some point. Therein is the solution. Those who succeed in healing the marriage return to their younger selves and become leaders again, or for the very first time—and they make this their primary committed endeavor for **twelve months**. They choose to think about the relationship like an investment and make sure they are taking care of it and themselves, not just sitting in the office playing with spreadsheets and optimizing until the next great liquidity event. Think being adventurous, fun, and engaging, not arguing, and stepping back into the positive cycle again.

"Remember that time we . . . Let's do that again. Not tonight? OK, tomorrow then. Let's do it." This is what they say to their wives on the daily. They worry about money less (or about the adventure to get more). They give up the chase—at least for a couple hours every day to give their wife attention, time, and energy. Because they actually care. And they show it.

Rich men work together with their spouse, not against them, and so their wife never wants to leave. He makes the marriage fun, not one of nagging commitment. He listens and takes feedback she offers. He hears it and does it, if it's reasonable, leaving ego out. What woman doesn't want to fully submit to a man like that?

Which brings us to the outcome of successfully passing the marital audit: The reward of a renewed marriage from the husband's perspective is **competent femininity**. What do I mean by this? It's similar to the difference between a "nice" guy and a *kind* guy, but it's the contrast between a "strong" woman and a *courageous* woman—it's that supporter-leader dynamic. She is happy with her man leading. He is responsible and capable of taking care of her, and so she goes out of her way to do things to please him.

Marriages fester into ruin when the high net worth husband abdicates, making her the leader of the household and the relationship. And so failing the audit—or failing to work to improve, in the event of failure—likely leads to divorce and financial ruin for the high net worth husband.

Some men, upon sensing their personal life entering a period of turmoil, ignore the wifely half of their equation. They dive headfirst into the quicksand pit of self-improvement. They become obsessed with improving themselves, from fitness to vices to personality flaws. This is not enough. The high net worth husband needs to retake the leadership role in his marriage, with the likeliest result being the flourishing of his wife into the ideal supportive spouse. The reward is worth the work.

What if it doesn't work out though? What then? We can be pragmatic. Remember Joe and Andrea? Stories like theirs end one of only two ways—and I've seen both. It's simple: They can fix it and do, or they don't and divorce. So what? Because the latter outcome presents the husband with an interesting situation. As long as he worked to pass as many of the marital audit tests as he could, and things didn't work out anyway, the divorce will likely be amicable and thus inexpensive. The next chapter explains how that will go.

By doing his best to pass the tests to improve his marriage, the high net worth man gives himself two ways to win and no ways to lose: Either he becomes the present, confident leader whose wife wants to give him a blowjob every day, or he finds a superior replacement who will.

Caution: The False Hope of Marriage Counseling

I'll close this chapter with a word of caution. Some couples, upon failing the marital audit, seek third-party support in the form of a marital counselor or therapist. This can do more harm than good. Often, marriage counseling is the wife's idea, and she feels as though she has to drag her husband along with her. Then during the session, the husband is reserved and standoffish, and the wife spends the session verbally berating him and getting the therapist onto her side. Everything wrong in the marriage is his fault, and the two-against-one dynamic confirms this.

Going into marriage counseling without a plan is, for the high net worth man, *retardio ad absurdum*. It's picking at a scab. It's poking the bear. It's anything but fun. And that's the energy that a couple who *will* one day sooner than later pass the marital audit has—fun. The marriage is fun again, or for the first time. And so this brief marriage counseling survival guide amounts to this: The man must take the lead, lay out the agenda, help his wife feel good, and make it a positive experience. It's all about energy, emotion, feeling. Even if the wife just vents, he cannot; he must hold frame, so to speak, allowing her to get the negativity out without resistance. She must be allowed to let it go. Then when it's gone, it's gone, and her husband is still there. It is rare that marriage counseling works, but when it does, it's because the husband doesn't take it too seriously. The only reason he's there is to pay his wife time and attention—not to agree with her or to air his own grievances in front of an allegedly impartial third party (which the situation is not; the therapist always takes the wife's side, even if it's a man). It is not possible for marriage counseling itself to improve the marriage, as that is not its purpose; but it is possible for marriage counseling not to end the marriage. That is the choice.

So if the marriage counseling "works," it's because the husband used the experience as an active listening tool to allow his wife to feel heard. Counseling will then not need to go on for long. A few sessions should do it, if any more than one or two.

If the counseling "doesn't work," it's because the couple treated it like it could. Or, what the counseling does is accelerate the already-inevitable. Fortunately, provided that the husband did not lose frame with his wife in front of a third party, an inexpensive, amicable separation is now the next step.

CHAPTER 4

PLANNING THE INEXPENSIVE, AMICABLE DIVORCE

Divorce and family law was initially developed to solve seemingly simple issues, including:

- Dividing assets equally and fairly.
- Providing the divorced wife with income so she would not become a burden to the state.
- Determining parental decision-making rights by an objective third party, including how much time the children may spend with each parent.
- Ending the marriage on an appropriate timeline (and without cruel and unusual expense; no divorce needs to be a seven-year war).

Of course, stressful emotions come with the territory regardless of how smooth the legal process may be. And yes, there are complexities to every case. However, divorce itself is not that complicated. What makes it complicated is hate between the exes, with a burning desire to exact vengeance kindled unnecessarily. That is how to create expensive, hateful divorces.

The (smart) rich do divorce differently. Immediately after completing (and likely failing) the marital audit, they start preparing for two possible outcomes: either a great marriage, or a great divorce. But how? Let me tell you a story you won't read or hear often.

One of the widest eye-openers in my career was helping a couple named Jay and Rebecca through their divorce. Rebecca had been a stay-at-home mother for fifteen years at that point, caring for their four children, and Jay was the embodiment of an all-american entrepreneur and was also a Marine Corps veteran.

Where their story deviates from the norm is what they asked me for: verification that Jay's business was worth what they projected (which was a lot!) and that his income would indeed likely increase over the next several years. He also planned reinvestments into growth projects, taking on larger parts inventory and new suppliers to expand across North and Central America. What did they want my help for? I'd understand if Rebecca wanted a third party valuation, assuming Jay was undervaluing the business. This would be par for the marital course. But I didn't notice that dynamic from them. Besides, both Rebecca *and* Jay contacted me. Together.

"What's the catch?" I asked.

"No catch," they said. "We're happily divorcing."

Happily divorcing? How could that be possible? Over the next few months, I would find out. But first, a little backstory that I would later learn.

Several years prior to that first call together, Jay had reached the conclusion that his marriage was "pretty fucking bad," as he put it. His explanation for this on follow-up was that his and Rebecca's relationship as parents was ideal, but the romantic spark was gone. The flame had died out. This is a common issue with many couples, but neither party blamed the other. They were amicable at that stage, still married.

Realizing the impending fate of the marriage, Jay worked on the relationship. So did Rebecca. Both made considerable effort to make it "work," to communicate and be there for each other and go out of their way to do niceties for each other and everything they both thought a good couple that would surely stay married would do. And it didn't work. "Trying" made it worse, ironically, and strained their relationship as co-parents and brought undue hassle into the children's lives as they found themselves deprioritized. After years of taking precedence over their parents' marriage, the children were not about to be replaced. And so both Jay and Rebecca knew.

But it was Jay who knew first. He was a former Marine, after all, and so had planned from the beginning for the possibility that this marital rekindling might not work. So he prepared. How? Well, Jay recognized the importance of understanding his wife's (at that time) needs and her wants. He paid beyond-the-usual attention to what was important to Rebecca in their marriage. He also began gently asking her what was important to her if they were to separate. What Jay found was that it was important to Rebecca that she be respected as a great mom, that nothing would threaten her role in their children's lives. And if there were to ever be a divorce, it would be inexpensive and amicable. But that would largely be because she would always be taken care of—Jay would pay for whatever while she kept primary care of the children. But he would stay involved as a co-parent as he had already been, and so they would work together to better their children's future.

Notice how the conditions for success in Jay and Rebecca's (at that time) hypothetical divorce became outcome-driven rather than process-driven. Easing Rebecca's mind meant Jay learning—and giving her—what she wanted out of any eventual divorce. And so as long as Jay ensured she received that outcome, divorce would be inexpensive and amicable relative to alternatives.

Now, outcome-driven divorce planning is the opposite of matrimonial law. The law prescribes a specific solution to a specific problem; it's a blunt instrument that doesn't ask questions. Most often at the end of this process, there are two losers and no winner. The law offers a set formula for a warring husband and wife who can't agree to anything and therefore need an authoritative third party (read: a judge) to hold them accountable.

Jay and Rebecca did it different. And while their marriage didn't survive, their respectful relationship as co-parents did. As they had already discussed and agreed, Rebecca needed some key conditions met in the divorce. Specifically, these included a paid-off house and enough child support and alimony to ensure she could continue to homeschool their children and afford a comfortable lifestyle with them. She had no interest in "the business," which she viewed as Jay's. It was important to keep the company intact for the children's future financial needs anyway.

All of Rebecca's needs and wants were easily met within their postnuptial agreement and eventual divorce. And by the way, the real reason she and Jay reached out to me for the second opinion on Jay's business and income was for his benefit—she worried she would receive *too much* in the divorce and put Jay's business at risk.

Happily divorced.

The Persuasive Power of the Postnuptial Agreement

What Jay did any high net worth individual can do, provided they do it while goodwill between spouses still exists. And that is to write a postnuptial agreement—*after* hearing from the other spouse what, specifically, they want in it so they'll be willing to sign it.

Now, this introduces several factors that go into *how* the rich divorce inexpensively and amicably. There is:

- Discussing the possibility of divorce.
- Deciding what terms are acceptable, in the event divorce becomes an inevitability.
- Drafting it all into a postnuptial agreement both spouses review with independent counsel and then sign.

We'll cover all three here. But first, what exactly is a postnuptial? Well, as you might guess, it's like a prenuptial agreement . . . for what happens after the spouses get divorced, not after the couple gets married. Postnuptials outline expectations as to what happens if the parties split. How will alimony be calculated? Division of assets? How will we have it be mediated? If mediation doesn't work, will we then go to binding legal arbitration instead of straight to trial? The post-nuptial agreement is a legally binding document. More like a shareholder agreement. "If we're to divorce, this is how."

A postnuptial agreement can be drafted by couples who had a pre-nuptial agreement or those who didn't; the point is to address changes in circumstances. It essentially overwrites the prenuptial agreement, if there was one. I once had a client whose prenuptial agreement took so long to pull together during the engagement, and it took so long for his fiancé to finally agree to it, that by the time it was signed, it technically became a postnuptial agreement.

Consider the timing of the postnup; it takes effect after separation, *not* the divorce. Even happily married couples have a postnuptial agreement; it pulls the couple out of a process designed to be painful and unclear and places them on a path that is more transparent with the outcome largely decided in advance—even if they never need to walk that path. A proper postnuptial ensures that the terms of the divorce are decided in advance, meaning both parties have an assurance they will not try to screw each other over. This eliminates any game-playing that both men and women do when trying to "stick it" to their ex.

Now, as a legally binding document, in order for it to hold up in divorce, both parties need to disclose *everything*. Any hidden assets, undeclared income, and so on must be disclosed. If the ex finds out about any of that later, it can be used to throw out the postnup and subject the divorce to that typical fifty-fifty down-the-middle divorce.

As you might imagine, many husbands get control-freakish in the postnup drafting process. Any domestically held assets in the husband's name with an easily accessible paper trail that are left out from the process leaves the postnup null and avoid. (Notice my strategic use of language; nothing written in that sentence negates Chapter 2.)

How then is the secretive or tempted-to-be-secretive spouse going to get the other party to sign a postnup, much less bring it up without that very conversation ending the marriage on the spot? Obviously, saying, "I want to protect myself in the event we divorce. Sign this," is not going to work. The postnup must be sold by the more motivated party as a form of security for the marriage. It should be presented as a way to protect the business, the investments, and the wealth for the children's sake, keeping the business out of the divorce. Then, concessions can be made else-where. Instead of spending hundreds of thousands of dollars and years fighting, the spouse can offer to pay for everything so that both parties can get what they want. The other spouse gets to be taken care of, and the business owner gets to keep the business running (in the context that a business valuation is typically split down the middle fifty-fifty in divorce, which usually means it has to be sold). Postnups only work when there is still goodwill in the relationship; there must be some genuine mutual respect for this to be floated.

The approach should be along the lines of, "Let's both invest in this relationship to fix it; but I want you to know that if this doesn't work, you will be taken care of. Your needs will be met, and you will feel secure. Let's talk about it."

A postnup is *always* worth it for HNW and UHNW couples. Their drafting costs typically only $5,000 or so. That said, the more complex the financial situation, and the more back and forth between spouses' lawyers there is, the higher that number rises. The highest I've personally worked on cost $40,000, but millions upon millions of dollars were at stake. It typically takes two to three months to complete a postnup though, and the process is faster for better marriages and slower for worse ones. Or in some cases, the marriage ends before the postnup is finished.

Alright. That's enough of the background. What's in these things?

The Essential Postnuptial

An above-board postnup agreement includes these sections and addresses the following questions and concerns:

- **Basic Financial**
  - What assets are separate versus marital
  - What liabilities are separate versus marital
  - How are marital assets and liabilities divided between the parties (business, house, investments, etc.)
- **Business-Related Issues**
  - What is the value of the business?
  - How is this value established? Following a set formula versus a gray-area opinion
  - Is the business a separate asset or marital asset?

- **Income Related Issues**
  - How to calculate income of the business owner for alimony and support purposes—a set formula
  - How is alimony calculated based on this income?
- **Divorce Procedures**
  - Collaborative, mediation, or binding arbitration?
  - Good-behavior clause (aka Non-Disparagement Clause) regarding husband and wife as well as children, family, friends, and colleagues
  - Set timelines for disclosure, and eventually, divorce
  - Set procedure for tying everything up in a tight little bow and sealing the deal

That's a little on what to do with a postnup. Now, for what *not* to do . . .

How to Botch a Postnup

I've seen these before. I'll probably see them again.

- When trying to set child support and custody, a parent can't waive the rights of their children. Inserting such a clause may void the entire contract.
- The agreement must be written, not verbal, and both spouses must receive independent legal counsel. Failure to ensure this could result in the agreement being void.
- If the outcome is overwhelmingly unfair to one party such as, *She gets nothing, I keep everything*, the judge will override the agreement.
- Coercion or duress can also void the agreement. Examples include:
  - Threatening divorce if the spouse doesn't sign.
  - Offering a financial benefit in exchange for signing.
  - Setting a time limitation to sign.
  - Introducing alcohol or drugs into the equation.
- Credible allegations of marital tort, such as abuse (e.g., physical, psychological, emotional, or financial) can lead to the entire agreement being void.

. . . .

By the way, adding their story to the book, I reached back out to Jay and Rebecca to check in. Several years had passed since the divorce finalized, had anything changed? How was it?

In short, great. Business is booming. Jay and Rebecca live on the same street. Co-parenting is simple, and the kids travel back and forth freely. Jay is involved with homeschooling, teaching his children business skills. Jay lives with his fiancé, Rebecca never remarried, and the three are at peace with each other. Rebecca receives far more in alimony and child support now, which Jay volunteered as his income increased; he wants his children to live well. Their family unit is still together, and everyone has adjusted well compared to normal divorce cases I encounter where lots of money (and the children) are up for debate.

CHAPTER 5

WHAT HAPPENS WHEN IT HAPPENS

U p to this point, the focus point of this book has been about planning ahead. If you're reading this book after your client—or you—have been served divorce papers, the great news is the next several chapters are specifically written with your urgency in mind.

In most of the cases I've dealt with, the high net worth man has been completely blindsided by divorce. Call it oblivious, or call it willful blindness, it doesn't matter. The husband thought he was holding up his end of the deal, only to find that his wife thought otherwise. Regardless, it's now time to look ahead and build the case to win. But how? What is the road ahead? What does winning even look like?

On a sunny April afternoon, I took a call from an eventual consulting client, Peter, who like many men wasn't prepared for the reality shock of divorce.

"What should I do?" he asked me the ten-million-dollar question.

"It depends. I need to know what happened first," I said.

Over the next two hours, Peter outlined the various trials and tribulations of the marriage and what precipitated the divorce proceedings. Peter, for his part, kept asking me "what to do" until finally discussing what went wrong.

Peter was a successful man in his mid-forties with an unusually profitable business for his industry. His wife, Sarah, was loosely associated with the business and was otherwise a stay-at-home mother to their teenage children. Peter, as it turns out, had recently "celebrated" becoming a new father . . . of a new child . . . from a different woman . . . who was much younger.

"So what?" I said.

"What do you mean?" Peter said, taken aback. "I cheated. This is all my fault."

"So what?"

It didn't register. I had to explain.

Playing Divorce to Win

"Winning" in family law, contrary to what some experts might tell you, is not a black-and-white outcome. Because here are two outcomes that will probably never happen (although the second outcome is in fact far likelier in practice):

1)   The husband keeps everything, the wife gets nothing.
2)   The wife keeps everything, the husband gets nothing.

That said, every outcome in between is possible, including both parties ending up with nothing and their respective attorneys ending up with new summer homes—and new boats.

Here's what winning *does* look like:

1)   Divorce as quickly as possible
2)   At as little cost as possible
3)   With assets as in-tact as possible
4)   As amicably as possible.

This is complete and total victory, and HNW and UHNW individuals play to that objective as best they can. Now, "best" varies because the parties vary. No two ex-wives are alike, but there are types. And how to handle the divorce in order to win it is based largely on who that woman is (again, I am speaking for the vast majority of high net worth marriages in which the husband is the successful businessman and the wife is the stay-at-home parent and part-time or no-income earner. This is not a book for edge cases, outliers, and exceptions, although my perspective for men is equally useful to women in the ultra-rare situation in which roles are reversed. But again, rare. (Women usually don't become billionaires except via a man, namely their father or husband, no matter what the Kardashians say.)

So, what is the strategy that empowers rich men to win their divorce? *It depends*.

On what? On playing the opponent, not the cards. Here are the four opponents.

The Four Archetypes of Ex-Wives

Who the high net worth man is divorcing determines his approach to the proceedings. Here are the four most common types of women I've encountered in divorce law when millions to billions were at stake.

1. The Peaceful, Settlement-Oriented Wife

This woman doesn't want to worry about anything. She is amicable. She wants her and the children to be taken care of. Security is her key leverage point. Thus, she avoids conflict even to her own detriment, if only for the promise of greater security and safety. Chapter 6 on alternative dispute resolution (ADR) is useful on how to handle this dynamic with ease and speed.

2. The Fair-Share Wife

Typically a business professional or at least experienced in the corporate environment, this woman "knows her rights." She is familiar with the law and thus pushes all the way to trial to get "her fair share." Her key leverage point is fairness. The way to beat this ex at her own game is covered in multiple chapters, from playing mind games with her to win, to defeating her lawyer at trial. Look at Chapters 7, 8, and 10 for how to manage ex-wife archetype number-two.

3. The Want-It-All Wife

She wants everything and is willing to fight for it. Nothing is ever enough for her in divorce; nothing was good enough for her in the marriage. Typically, she has a history of berating her husband, cheating on him (then blaming him), scorning her husband for sexual intimacy (until he cheats), or all three and more. She goes to court to win at all costs and is known for feeling "betrayed," to use her favorite word. Her key leverage point is creating the perception she has won through the appearance of justice and satiation of her revenge craving. Chapters 8, 10, and 11 will be helpful.

4. The Public Want-It-All Wife

This woman is all of archetype number-three except she is a public figure in her own right or otherwise focuses on her image and tries to keep up appearances. Her reputation is thus her key leverage point. In particular, Chapter 11 will be helpful in vanquishing her rage.

• • • •

Situation decides strategy. The first two archetypes are usually dealt with best in divorce via ADR, specifically collaborative or mediation, sometimes arbitration with tougher cases. With the latter two, however, these women want everything from their husbands leaving him with nothing, so ADR *never* works for. (Skip right to Chapter 7 if you are in urgent need of wisdom on how to respond to their baseless accusations and cruel and unusual divorce demands.)

There are two litigation streams, the first of which (ADR) works for the first two archetypes. But the latter, leading to a trial and ruling by a judge, is where the category three and four ex-wives want to bring their men kicking and screaming. It is formal and warlike. There are truths. There are facts. There is evidence. Courts rely on evidence. The rest don't matter. But evidence can mean anything it is made to mean.

As you can see, the path a successful divorce takes is decided in advance of the divorce itself. High net worth individuals don't take the path that won't end well; they don't play games they have low odds of winning. Therefore, what works for some in the chapters ahead won't work for others.

But for all four ex-wives, there is one catch-all that *can* work to win the divorce for the husband. It works almost every time it's tried. Even then, "almost" is hedging; it's never *not* worked when I've advised clients or my clients' clients to use it. This sure way to win is called:

The Best Offer That Wins

What I call **The Best Offer** is the settlement offer the husband makes to his wife at any point in the divorce or prior, whether in the middle of the trial or long before, way back up to and including the postnuptial conversation. It works.

The Best Offer is precisely that—it is the maximum offer the man is willing to pay to get this over with. Usually, for wealthy individuals, it is, at minimum, seven figures. The man knows his income, his net worth, and his business valuation. What is he willing to pay to protect it? It must be enough to persuade even the fourth archetypal wife. She must be able to bring the offer to her lawyer and he tells her, "Take it."

With The Best Offer, the husband wins and his wife wins—a little. The extreme alternative is divorce by trial, and both man and woman lose.

Is a one-time seven-figure payment plus additional biweekly or monthly payments still a victory? Yes. Because seven-figure legal fees are not uncommon when the divorces of the wealthy make it to trial. The Big Offer is already a savings relative to the alternative. A trial alone is $30,000 per day for fifteen days minimum. It's also a second job, from before the divorce is filed until after its completion. Opportunity cost and attention investment must be considered. The Best Offer is thus best for both the man and his wife. The exact amount is a question of what the wife believes the man is worth, what alimony will sustain the current lifestyle, and what child support provides for the kids. From the man's perspective, anything less than fifty-fifty is a win (for him) because that's better than the eventual court case amount *and* without seven figures in legal fees. So 40 percent of wealth (in the case of, for example, a $10 million business and a $4 million settlement offer), is a win. Relatively a win, but a win regardless. Again, there is no reality where the ex leaves the marriage with nothing, except in the case of a legally valid prenuptial agreement. But in my experience, only about two-thirds of prenups are legally valid.

Now, the husband's Best Offer must indeed be high by his wife's standards—and yet no higher. This is a common issue with men, more common than "skimping" on that first settlement offer. Why? Psychology.

Unforced Errors and the Power of Guilt

Lust makes men do stupid things. So, too, does guilt. Recall Peter from the outset of this chapter. Peter's case was no different than many cases for other high net worth men. He made a (baby-sized) error, and the Divorce was conceivably his "fault." Naturally, he felt guilty. Men bear the weight of guilt much more heavily than women do even for the same sin, based on my professional experience dealing with both parties. Women may feel guilty, but that emotional state doesn't noticeably impact their decision making in the divorce. Women play to win and play very hard. She may have had an affair with her husband's brother, father, *and* best man, and she will *still* become the fourth wife archetype and play to win (true story).

Men, however, feel guilty and play to tie. And then lose, quite badly, whether that's at trial or with a Best Offer—more like a Too Good Offer, and it's something like sixty-forty her/him with regard to division of assets. Not even the most misandrist judge would grant such an outcome in a no-fault divorce state. And yet men will do it if they feel guilt, shame, and remorse over their behavior.

What they must understand is that the marriage is over. Who is to blame doesn't matter. Blame is a social construct anyway, not a legal construct in a no-fault divorce world (i.e., nobody is at fault, even the person who *was* at fault). Recall that the best outcome for the man, his children, and soon-to-be-ex-wife is to:

1) Divorce as quickly as possible
2) At as little cost as possible

3) With assets as in-tact as possible
4) As amicably as possible.

The best way is to win. And so the man must accept that he did some things that feel "wrong." He must also accept that his instincts to "tie" with his wife are just as wrong. He must accept that being submissive didn't help the marriage and it won't help in the divorce either (in my experience, many HNW and UHNW men had "man caves" in their home, as well as mentally and emotionally throughout their lives, those rare few spaces where the wife allowed him to be himself; the dynamic was not one of harmony but combativeness, her against him until he retreated into his own spaces and checked out of the marriage entirely). Furthermore, the man must accept that he may need to be ruthless at times for the good of his family and conciliatory at other times, also for the good of those he loves. This is war. It will destroy his soul if he lets it. What happens if he doesn't?

Let's look to Peter.

Based on his case history, we pushed Peter directly into the admittedly costly, emotional, and tolling litigation stream immediately (see how this can play out, in Chapter 8). We also trained Peter to play to win. And so he played ruthless and hardball. After some coaxing, he was positioned in the driver's seat of litigation for most of the process. The divorce went where he took it, for his benefit. Soon we sensed his vindictive wife Sarah had softened up. Or perhaps she'd been worn down. Or both. Then came The Big Offer, and she accepted prior to what would have been a lengthy, costlier trial. We also skipped other stages we knew would not have worked for Sarah. She was not the ADR type. And so Peter avoided a nearly guaranteed-to-fail collaborative law attempt ($50,000 savings) as well as a likely failed mediation attempt (another $50,000 or more in savings). And, of course, we avoided a long, drawn-out, merciless, and soul-destroying process in which Sarah could have crushed Peter into the ground (priceless). The settlement Sarah accepted was (far) less than Peter's possible exposure to loss at trial. It abated Sarah so well, by the way, that the divorce ended better than it had begun; the couple went from bitter enemies to friendly speaking terms.

That's a win.

CHAPTER 6

HOW THE RICH COLLABORATE AND MEDIATE TO DIVORCE

The Best Offer is the quickest and cleanest way through a divorce. However, it comes with two major drawbacks, namely:

1) It only works with certain archetypal exes (i.e., the settlement-oriented and sometimes the fair-shares).
2) The Best Offer requires trust.

Fortunately for the divorce law industry—and unfortunately for many divorcing rich couples—the present-day state of male versus female dynamics (especially so on social media) has spread the communicable disease of distrust between men and women on the whole. Up this ante with the fact that women have become professionally oriented, shifting many women out of the settlement-oriented ex-wife role into another, more combative archetype.

Divorces have become more contentious, costlier, and longer; palpable distrust of one another has become the default starting point in many cases. Alternative Dispute Resolution (ADR) was originally introduced to the divorce industry as a way to bring the stalemate between the sexes to a ceasefire. As we covered in Chapter 5, ADR includes:

- **Mediation**
- **Collaboration**
- **Arbitration**

Whichever way you take it, ADR is generally a more affordable and flexible way to avoid the high costs of litigation (except when it's not; more on that shortly). In **mediation**, the spouses, usually each represented by a lawyer, hire a third lawyer (the mediator) to help reach a negotiated settlement. This settlement is flexible but generally aligns with standard legal guidelines; any settlement offer deemed too far away from those guidelines (e.g., a seventy-thirty split of marital assets) is immediately rejected, if not never proposed in the first place. Mediation can be effective for certain personalities, as discussed in Chapter 5.

Then there's **collaborative** family law; it's pricier than mediation initially and for good reason—more people are involved and need to be paid. In collaboration, both spouses have their own lawyer (of course), but they pull together a team that often includes a joint family therapist and a financial professional, sometimes a divorce coach or other professionals considered helpful to reaching a mutually agreeable settlement. The team "collaborates" to gather financial data, calculate support payments, help establish a budget, keep both parties calm, cool, and collected, and so on. Collaboration approach is less adversarial and encourages quick, amicable resolutions—for the right couple. You can imagine how a collaborative divorce is particularly beneficial for business owners who may need creative solutions for issues like cash flow and property division.

Finally there's binding **arbitration**, which involves a neutral third party (the arbitrator) who listens to both sides and then makes decisions on the disputed issues. These decisions are legally binding and enforceable much like a divorce court ruling and cannot be appealed. Arbitration is "litigation lite" and lets a couple feel like they're "fighting it out" without the expense of actual litigation and stress of a real trial.

Rich divorcees who retain their riches post-marriage understand what they're getting themselves into with ADR. Mediation and collaboration both involve two spouses who are not willing to fight each other; arbitration is two spouses willing to fight but only passive-aggressively. ADR is the stream taken when the HNW or UHNW individual recognises that that is their best play, for they are playing the person (their ex) not just playing the game of high-stakes divorce.

So regardless of ADR type selected, I advise clients and my clients' clients in these situations to aim for a lump-sum settlement on alimony, support, or property, if possible, with no ongoing payments. This financially disconnects the exes completely and also avoids future reassessments of income or business value that could loom over those required biweekly or monthly payments.

Now, earlier I mentioned that ADR does not always work. Why does it not always work? Because while ADR is typically seen as a quicker and cheaper option, its effectiveness depends on the cooperation of the spouses. With a vindictive spouse, usually the wife, ADR can end up being more expensive and drawn out as she may use the process to prolong conflict and create financial uncertainty. Thus, the wealthy individual with the type three or type four wife—the want-it-all or the public want-it-all—skips ADR altogether. They understand they are dealing with a vengeful woman bent on raising melodramatic hell and draining assets as fast as she can for as long as she can. Some type two ex-wives may engage in this behavior as well; she *claims* to just want her fair-share, as she whines to the mediator or arbitrator, meanwhile she makes demands of her husband that he will never agree to settle on, and that's the point. Fairness, in this case, is not equal income or assets, it's equal pain.

Let me tell you a story.

A Tale of Two ADR Couples

I met Jonathan and Alexandra fairly early in my career; this divorcing couple was by any account the model pair for mediation. Jonathan was a successful businessman with a consistent earning history, and Alexandra was a professional by trade but had opted to become a stay-at-home mother some years prior to divorce.

I recognized Alexandra immediately as the classic type two archetype; she wanted to make sure everything was covered so she and the kids got what was "fair." Jonathan, for his part, was mostly an open book and wanted to move on and get this thing over with.

Jonathan and Alexandra had decided, upon separation, to attend mediation in an attempt to resolve any possible disputes arising from their eventual divorce. As in any divorce, there are emotions involved and hurt feelings, even when neither party is directly responsible for the shriveling of the marriage. In Jonathan and Alexandra's case, there was no specific cause. And maybe that's really what happened. The passion dried up, and that was that.

So Jonathan and Alexandra bickered back and forth in mediation (about how much his business was worth and his earnings) but settled with the second offer, Jonathan's Next-Best Offer. This was in their first mediation. Day-of settlement. No reservations. After some work to prove to Alexandra that the business was not worth as much as she thought and that his income would not be as high going forward as much as she wanted, of course. Since the angle we took was "getting your fair share" for Alexandra, she had an energy of openness rather than vindictiveness.

Then there were Michael and Christine. Their setup was effectively identical. Michael was, at the time, a busy and successful entrepreneur. Christine was, you guessed it, also a professional, who'd become a stay-at-home mother and had been so for over a decade.

And that's where their similarities with Jonathan and Andrea end— and why many attempts at Alternative Dispute Resolution invariably fail. In contrast to Jonathan and Alexandra, there was a flashpoint that precip-itated the divorce: an affair.

It was bad.

Christine presented as the worst-case type three. This jaded ex-wife had to "take everything," and that was her only option. In mediation, no offer was ever good enough. She needed more. In second mediation, exactly the same thing happened. Then because Michael ignored my con-sultative advice (which was to go straight to trial), he tried mediation a THIRD time.

Surprise! It failed. Four years and $200,000 later, Michael was back to square one and was rapidly depleting assets to pay for it all. For his efforts, Michael now got to experience a long and contentious divorce process that took approximately eight more years and way more money. This experience was made far worse by the failed mediation attempts.

With every failure, both parties became more entrenched and dug into their positions. Christine wanted to burn it all down, and mediation just added fuel to her fire.

This is exactly what happens in failed ADR attempts, by the way. Frustrations mount (sometimes by a vindictive spouse's design), and the eventual litigation becomes far worse for the party who just wants it all to be done.

The sad end to this story is that twelve years later, Michael won at trial and ended up in a position where Christine owed him substantial money. But Christine couldn't pay—and will likely never be able to. Michael's only recourse is that he just doesn't need to pay anymore. A big loss.

Now, I'm guessing that many of you are indirectly rationalizing this loss because of the affair.

"It's his fault!"

"He deserves it!"

No, Michael didn't deserve it. His ex-wife may have been vengeful, but this was a no-fault divorce case. She just wanted to take everything he had and destroy him.

Oh, right . . . I nearly forgot. She's the one who had the affair.

I'll say it one more time: *You don't play the game, you play the person.* With that orientation, the smart rich do what it takes to get their best victory, which is opened up or constrained by their ex's character, personality, and so forth. The strategy is no strategy but the best path to victory (with acceptable losses) in their unique situation. *Which option is the best available?* This is opposed to the stance taken by *low* net worth people who believe "she won't get anything" and resist prudence at every stage until the trial is concluded and their ex is entitled to, as it often goes, 60 percent or more of the marital assets.

The wealthy and wise divorce with pragmatism. They will take either path they must, ADR or litigation. They are always willing to play the game within the game—the mind games. This mini-game can be entered (or thrust upon the individual) on either path at any time. They deserve their own separate chapter before we continue with the divorce process, specifically the process and expectations of litigation. Mind games may be necessary if heels are dug in, particularly with the burn-it-all-down, make-'em-suffer type of spouse. A little mental play can reposition that individual so they feel their position backsliding—and it becomes easier to settle, be that in ADR, in litigation, all the way up to prior to trial. In the context of winning, mind games are legally permissive and ethically ambiguous. To improve the position of a client in a divorce, there are certain tactics that are wildly out-of-bounds. But there are those which may not be "nice" and yet work. Playing mind games to win is just that.

CHAPTER 7

PLAYING MIND GAMES TO WIN

Playing mind games and controlling the narrative in divorce cases go hand-in-hand. This reality is often overlooked if not rejected due to the false assumption that "the truth" will shine through. It won't. The reality is that whoever pushes their ex to exclaim, completely exasperated, "Just send the papers already; I'll sign them!" has won. More often than not among the wealthy, it is the ex-wives who are playing to win and the ex-husbands who are desperate for an end to what feels like psychological torture. The smart rich men handle mental warfare differently.

Let me tell you about Sean and Shelly. I was approached by Shelly in the latter stages of her divorce with her soon-to-be-ex-husband Sean. Shelly entered this divorce under the presumption that she had a winning hand. However, what became abundantly clear is that neither Shelly (a practicing physician) nor her attorney had a handle on Sean. I recognized what was really going on. But by that point, Shelly was desperate to just be done with it all. She was an intelligent and prominent woman yet was suffering from full-blown cold-sweat nightmares about her divorce case as well as anxiety attacks with each and every email notification. Her attorney was dazed and confused. Why?

Because Sean was a professional negotiator—literally. He was the head of mergers and acquisitions at a large US investment bank. He knew what to do. For example, Sean would offer to meet for coffee with Shelly amid the divorce proceedings. He would show up, sometimes, as "Happy

Sean." Other times, he would no-show or cancel at the last second without excuse, explanation, or apology. Sean would also communicate that he was preparing to settle. Then he would ghost everyone. Days later, after no replies to messages, he would remerge and demand a trial. He seemed to make no sense whatsoever.

Sean would attend mediation, agree to key sections of a proposed settlement in the negotiation, then find himself suddenly called out "for an urgent business meeting." When Shelly's attorney would later send the agreement prepared and discussed in that same mediation, Sean would refuse signing it, even agreeing to it. Then, days later, Sean would say that he'd be willing to work with the old agreement, not the new one. "Send me the old agreement. I'll review with my lawyer, and sign it," he said. Then "his lawyer" had issues with the agreement. Back to square one again.

Millions of dollars on the line. Almost there, now gone, rinse and repeat.

I want to be clear: Sean was never cruel, unpleasant, or unkind, at least outwardly. But this game was hardcore mental warfare and had brought Shelly on the brink of a breakdown. Sean wasn't stressed at all.

Some negotiations really do involve cruel, unpleasant, and unkind negotiators. Such was the case with José and Mary. José is a recent consulting client of mine who approached me to assist in guiding his contentious and difficult divorce proceedings with his wife, Mary.

José ran several profitable businesses and appeared to be fairly calm and level-headed in spite of the surrounding circumstances. However, when dealing with his ex, he became understandably emotional and upset.

Mary had made some fairly bold and vile accusations of wrongdoing by José. The details aren't important overall, but if you listened to Mary, you'd be under the impression that José belonged in jail for a very long time. José denied these claims completely. The police investigated and found no evidence of wrongdoing. But Mary continued on regardless.

The major issue Jose was facing at that point was Mary drove the narrative of the case. All his time was spent trying to put out her fires, replying in detail in an attempt to dismiss or discredit each salacious claim of hers. This left no time to offer his competing (and accurate) version of events.

Working with José was a matter of getting his emotions under control and persuading him to start setting the narrative rather than defending himself constantly from Mary's. Emotional self-regulation is so essential to successful divorce, particularly among high-performing men. Every time men like José respond emotionally—even to blatantly false accusations—they indirectly accept their ex-spouse's mischaracterization of them. This is via actions, which speak louder than words. Mary had accused José of, among other things, emotional abuse. So when José *acted* emotional in his denial of her claims, he was behaving in accordance with Mary's narrative—reacting with negative emotion. It was thus easy to "see" José acting just the way Mary claimed he had, but in private, and also doing far worse.

José needed a change.

Two Mind Games

Mental games can be played at any point at any stage of divorce. They work in ADR (Chapter 6) and in litigation (Chapter 8), so consider this topic a natural bridge between the two.

Now, mind games are played to get the other person on the same page; done correctly, mind games come across as nudging, not forcing, as gently pulling, not violently pushing. And there are two types of mind games to play.

Playing Mind Games with the Ex

There are several mind games to play against the other party. This is not an exhaustive list but an essential one of the most useful.

Frames and Reframes

A *frame* is an interpretation; a *reframe* is a reinterpretation. Frames and reframes are used for narrative control and thus—most importantly—**persuasion**. Reframing presents an alternative reality that explains the facts and offers a new meaning that is more beneficial to the party deploying this narrative control tactic.

For example, the claim against an ex-husband such as, "He doesn't spend any time with me and the kids. He's always at work!" could be reframed as, "I took time out of my day to spend time with you and invest in the children. Here are pictures of us on vacation, at the park," etc. This reframe is a superior claim that completely dismantles and debunks the prior accusatory claim and has evidence to support it (ideally including pictures and specific dates).

Effective reframing makes the other party doubt their own version of events, as they're relying on just a feeling as opposed to the hard facts presented by the reframer. Reframing inserts uncertainty on their side that they will be taken seriously, which their lawyer notices as well.

This reframing can be used throughout the process—before, during, and after ADR, a trial, etc. Ideally, reframing should begin even *before* separation. The best way to do this—documenting the facts to disprove feelings—would be via email or text, as that provides the actual proof. And it should be done matter-of-factly, not combatively.

Now, reframing intended to weaken the other party's position is deployed in a relationship headed for or already in the midst of divorce. It is *not* to be used when repair is possible. Active listening, validation, and collaboration towards solutions are essential to salvage or improve a marriage. But in a divorce situation, invalidation is the objective, as the reframer's version of events is what must win out.

For more on this subject, Scott Adams has an excellent book titled "Reframe your Brain" which has dozens of reframes to Stay Rich and lead a better life.

Urgency and Scarcity

Serving offers that need to be replied to very quickly, such as giving an offer with a twenty-four-hour reply deadline, is a tactic used in divorce negotiations. Nobody can get back in time for something like that to conduct a proper review. This specific example of deployed urgency and scarcity is known as "running out the clock," and the intent is not for the offer to be accepted. But it gets better; then the next "almost settled" offer is presented, with millions of dollars at stake and "just one thing to tweak." However, when the other party responds, there is no response from the initial offering party—and the negotiation goes back to square one. This process is repeated over and over, with enticing offers that have one last little hurdle to overcome. Now, there is usually something really obviously off about the offer, like the settlement amount from the husband is oddly high but sole custody is demanded—that's not going to work. Obviously she won't accept it. Such offers are designed to fail. But what they work to do is <u>demoralize</u> the other party. And that does work.

Here's an actual example with numbers: The real amount an ex-wife should have been awarded in a divorce settlement was $5 million. However, urgency and scarcity pushed her to accept a much lower number, just to get it over with. She thought, as far as I could tell, *I'll take two million because. I just can't deal with this anymore. I just want him to sign a settlement. I just need to get this over with.*" The urgency and scarcity play cost more time and money—perhaps $100,000 in legal fees over an additional two months—but it saved the offering party $3 million in the settlement.

This happens more than you might like to think.

Intermittent Uncertainty

Ex-wives tend to play this mind game well, particularly when children are involved. Here's a real-life example I happen to be familiar with: The ex-wife would have the couple's kids, then bring them over to the ex-husband's place with last-minute notice on a day he was not scheduled to have them, completely disrupting his plans. She would also sign up the kids for a multi-weeklong summer activity the same week he was supposed to have them, which makes the ex-husband be "the bad guy" if he demands the kids spend those weeks with him. The result of this intermittent uncertainty is that he will do just about anything to be with his kids. His ex-wife likes that. It's cruel. It works. It works because it's cruel.

Now, the way to play this mind game right back is to not let it be played in the first place. That is hard to do, frankly, because playing it works especially well over time (months and years). The ex-wife can keep doing it and make it worse. The intermittent uncertainty wears the other partner down over time; the more she plays it, the worse he gets at it.

Another example of playing intermittent uncertainty (for women) is to go from pleasant to angry and back again without warning. The man and his legal counsel are completely thrown off-guard. They don't know how to reason with a seemingly unreasonable person—and that's how she gets him.

For men, intermittent emotional uncertainty must be the sudden shifts from presence to absence. It's giving undivided positive attention, then withholding all attention, then shifting back again, all without any obvious explanation. Note that anger doesn't work for men as it does for women, as any display of rage from a man supports his wife's narrative that he is a narcissistic, sociopathic abuser. A game men can play is to pay alimony but not child support, or the other way around. Or to make an unwritten demand before releasing one or the other (or both). Any and all tactics to grind the other party down.

The Best Offer, Revisited

Persuasive offer design is key to successful divorce negotiation. Negotiation happens throughout the process, and it is a *process*, not a single event.

When making an offer, the persuading party must state explicitly what each section means. Throwing numbers around means nothing. Spell it out. Paint a picture. Show, don't tell. The persuading party would use phrases like, "What this lump-sum alimony settlement means is a lifestyle with security and safety, and you'll be able to benefit immediately rather than wait years and years for small, slow-drip installments."

Isn't this the obvious way to go about settlement offer negotiation? Well, yes, but few do it (so they lose big). This is because legal counsel is often concerned with getting the numbers right, above all else. But the shrewd divorcing businessperson is able to alternate between "math brain" and "story brain."

A persuasive best offer together with the other mind games to play with the other party are only persuasive if they are cloaked. The appearance of good-faith negotiation must remain. If manipulation is obvious, it is immediately rendered ineffective, particularly at trial. Let's talk about that next.

Playing Mind Games at Trial

Storytelling is the longest mind game to play and also the most effective as you become the more credible party in the relationship (with the right story). This matters most leading up to and during the trial itself. **The best storyteller always wins**—and the rich tell rich stories.

Storytelling is the primary way in which knowledge has been passed from generation to generation throughout the existence of mankind. Becoming an adept storyteller is a life skill. The use of pauses, language changes, tone changes, etc. can all be crafted in a way to maximize the impact of certain points in a story. But here, we are just at the outset of litigation, so this isn't so much about a "story" as it is "a narrative."

The high net worth negotiator needs to develop and stick to a credible and plausible narrative as to why things are the way they are. In doing so, he will deliver a logical framework on how to "view" the litigation, and as long as this frame sticks (mostly), the judge will be forced to accept (at least some of) his conclusions.

Rule #1 of any narrative is: Don't lie. But you can tell a story that suits your purpose. Namely, you want a narrative that supports:

- A lower income assessment and avoiding corporate income being "attributed" to the individual personally.
- A lower business valuation.

The bias of a business owner is to reduce income and the valuation, especially leading up to divorce and going into post-separation. This needs a *bona fide* reason to explain the decline in business, such as customer loss, lead slowdown, increased expenses, and earnings management. Personal goodwill can also be argued, such as having an easily replaceable product, no contracts in place, heavy reliance on one customer, etc.

The Western view of the world still largely adheres to the principle that men are the protectors and providers for the family unit and that women are largely innocent in divorce proceedings. This view is shifting with some rapidity but is still largely true in the judiciary, with some caveats. The man should be supporting the woman in achieving career- and life-oriented objectives, supporting the woman in decision-making for the family, being honest, open, communicative, thoughtful, etc., and being involved in the children's lives on an intimate and ongoing basis.

The willingness of courts to accept brazen and temperamental men is fairly low. Going fifty-fifty (split custody) is the starting point for custody rather than the woman having the kids most of the time. "Abuse" and "violence" are now far-reaching and exploratory terms, no longer limited to actual physical harm. It can be mental, emotional, or even financial (as in she doesn't have access to the bank accounts). Really, it can be portrayed as anything that displays a pattern of coercion. This is why the winning narrative has to:

- Rebut allegations of abuse and violence.
- Portray the man as a good and competent father and husband.
- Portray the man as even-headed, logical, and kind.

Easy ways to demonstrate the above qualities include:

- Providing evidence that he has supported his spouse and her career and life ambitions, such as paying off college debt, supporting her if she wanted to work somewhere else, refraining from *ad hominem* attacks, maintaining composure in all correspondence (text messages, phone calls, emails, in person), and peppering the record in emails and text messages with statements like "I want to support you," "The business isn't doing as well right now," "You're a great mother," etc.
- Rebutting allegations of abuse or violence by maintaining an even temperament, refraining from personal attacks and accusations, letting her make choices, keeping notes on arguments (who said what and why, writing down the things she said to use as evidence), and making sure she has access to any and all joint accounts.

There are a few powerful frames to install in a case narrative. Recall that divorces today (in most jurisdictions) are no-fault divorces, meaning that there is no real benefit to shoveling shit as the man in court. Powerful narratives include:

- "I am the husband and father of the children. I love my children and will always support them."
- "I am a reasonably successful business owner. Unfortunately, my wife really enjoyed spending money, so we lived beyond our means for a number of years."
- "I am ethical and competent. I let my accountant take care of the taxes—I know some parts but not all parts."
- "Any cash income earned I have deposited in our bank account or recorded as sales in the company."
- "I'm not burned or angry about the divorce and whatever she's done. I just want to get things over with and make sure she gets whatever is fair."

The above is what I suggest my clients tell others, including legal counsel. If he cheated, fine, who cares. Say it, own it, move on. "I know I made a mistake. I just want to get things over with and ensure she gets what is fair." His actions—including playing mental games to win—won't necessarily reflect this after the separation, but this is narrative-building.

I want my clients' full narrative, which will be brought up if this thing goes all the way to trial, to go something like this:

She and I were married on August 22th, 2010. We had a great life together and two kids who I adore. Luckily, I was able to earn enough that she's been able to stay home to care for the kids. She is a licensed physiotherapist who could start working really at any time.

This role would allow some flexibility with the kids, and I could support this transition, too. A part-time physiotherapist makes $52,500 in New York State. My ex has always been great with the kids. She's a wonderful mother, and I'll always love her for that.

I own a small but profitable IT consulting business. I had an office and a home office. Unfortunately, because of the divorce, I lost several clients as I was unable to maintain the demands of this work. It's been a very stressful time. My costs have increased substantially; I'm losing money everywhere. In fact, I hate to say it, but I admit I'm broke. Most of these clients come through personal and professional referrals. They come for my services, for me personally. I had great relationships in the past, but many of them have soured. I don't know if the business will ever recover.

I would always work long hours but took time out dedicated to the kids. I even would put my phone away to spend time with the kids and during family time. We took vacations together here and there; it was great. Then it happened. She became very volatile and would make a lot of threats and accusations. She pulled a knife on me once and threw dishes at me another time. It was a very scary and threatening environment, and that's why we've split. I just want what's best for the kids. I'm broke but will pay whatever is fair I can for the kids and to her. I sent several offers of settlement, and they were always rejected.

There could be a million other pertinent facts here, but this is what we want the narrative to look and sound like. As important and integral as the narrative is, shrewd negotiators find the evidence to support it. They document things—in email, on the computer, by text—throughout the relationship. Keep records and use them to support the narrative to be built.

Speaking of supporting a narrative, how did that ultimately go for Sean and José?

Well, Sean wasn't stressed. I pierced the veil and explained to Shelly that this was all a game, and the goal was to get a number that worked. We eventually got things done with a decent number Shelly could live on (and live with). As for Sean, he managed to walk away with a multi-seven-figure savings simply by playing games. They had agreed on the child aspect first, covering expenses like paying for private school and other ongoing costs. They also agreed on a lump-sum alimony payment, but the amount was 33 percent of what it "should" have been. Additionally, there were big savings on the equalization of property. Sean had played mind games with that, too—and won.

As for José, he needed to retake control of the narrative itself, reframing himself as the hero, not a villain. There were many unfounded and incorrect accusations about what he had done. He needed to get more emotionally self-regulated and tell his side of the story first, not just respond to Mary's. As we learned, he was spending too much time responding and not enough time telling his version of events, which he needed to do because she was psychologically abusive and had actually hit him—which she refused to admit. But as José started to reframe, he began to win.

For example, he pointed out that due to Mary's behavior, his businesses had begun to lose customers. He was doing the best he could to keep it all together. José also talked about how combative his wife had become, showing how he was trying to do his duty and that leaving the house was a way to diffuse the arguments she started. We showed that José had become a "superdad" whose wife had put him in a terrible position.

José won; he gained primary custody *and* control of the children and decisions involving them. Mary's original assertion was that his businesses were worth eight figures, between $20 and $30 million most likely. However, by taking control of the narrative, we were able to credibly bring that number down to less than $5 million. I helped José offer the most beneficial truth in order to knock down that valuation, and given the credibility we'd built for José before the judge at trial, it made sense to trust our side instead of Mary's.

Play mind games to win, and you win big.

CHAPTER 8

LITIGATION STRATEGY AND TACTICS

L et me tell you the story of the one that got away.

Marshall and Karen lived the swinging lifestyle, which didn't work out (as it usually doesn't), leading to their separation. Marshall was otherwise a serial entrepreneur with four health-food businesses, including a gluten-free (GF) business. During the divorce proceedings, Marshall claimed that the GF business was "out" and that the businesses were suffering and he had the numbers to prove it. He printed out all the financials and delivered them without page numbers, all out of order, without warning, in six boxes of paper. He essentially said, "There's the disclosure," creating a great effort for Karen to figure out what was going on, such as which business each document belonged to, whether an entry was an expense or revenue, and so on.

Marshall sold 30 percent of all his businesses to his friends and flipped his remaining shares into trusts that were expressly for the purposes of the children, making them discretionary, which meant he could decide when to withdraw or send money. He then took all the proceeds from the sales of that 30 percent to his friends (somewhere between $5 and $10 million total, to my estimate) and loaned it to his four companies, then had each company loan money to the other companies. On paper, it looked like the businesses were in massive debt to one another—and to him! This created so much complexity between and among the businesses, making it a total headache for Karen to argue against.

Even better, Marshall ran 100 percent of his personal expenses through the business and took those as deductions from his shareholder accounts so he was getting his money back, which counted as $0 income. The new minority owners (the 30 percent) also charged very high consulting fees, which punched the businesses into net loss positions, making the companies no longer profitable and thus having much lower on-paper valuations.

All of this came out during litigation and put Karen at a distinct disadvantage, even though ALL of this was provable and yet still legal. Karen was advised to accept a $500,000 settlement and $2,000 per month alimony before trial, as she was at her breaking point due to the financial web Marshall had created. The trial would have taken at least a month, and she just wanted it over with. The result from the trial was very uncertain, and there was a high chance that the judge could conclude that the husband had $0 income and businesses worth $0 since he had a way to make that argument credibly on paper. Ultimately, Karen decided to take the settlement offered. Marshall got away with everything he wanted from that litigation. If I'd known then what I knew now, perhaps he wouldn't have.

Introduction to Formal Litigation

Much of Marshall and Karen's story unfolded in the context of **formal litigation**. Formal litigation means filing for divorce with the court; the eventual result is either a settlement (before trial) or a trial in which a judge (and sometimes a jury, depending on the type of case and the jurisdiction) makes the final determination. Matrimonial law is predominantly judge-only, which on balance is a good thing despite whatever inherent biases a judge may have.

Now, formal litigation is a drawn-out, money-draining process. Generally, this is the highest conflict route of a proceeding. With a combative spouse, the high net worth can expect to land here, regardless of whether they want to or not. If they find themselves with such an ex, as I said earlier, they will proceed straight to formal litigation and avoid running up costs on ADR, which goes nowhere.

Assuming one party holds most of the assets in the divorce, there is a simple strategy that I've seen played time and again which can work: Bleed out the opponent. Recognize that lawyers, and especially matrimonial lawyers, do not work for free. Matrimonial lawyers are especially touchy about fees because they generally run up professional debt in higher proportions to other fields of law. They tend to expect large retainers and will stop working once the retainer is gone.

So the high net worth individual's role here is to fight everything that is reasonably arguable. If the other party is asking for too much information, they may make them file a motion in court. If there are issues with the kids, then file a motion in court. I advise my clients to engage in much correspondence with opposing counsel, as they tend to have time and the bankroll on their side, with most assets and accounts being in their name.

I also tell clients this: Do not sell the matrimonial home, or at least delay sales as long as possible (this frees up funds for the ex to fight). I don't want my clients to push anything too far, just to push to a reasonable limit. They may base levels of child support and alimony if they have to, but they should argue that their ex should be working. We include this in the calculation of whatever they're going to pay.

The shrewd divorce negotiator forces the other party to argue over minute little details, citing technicalities in the law. We wait a while to respond to anything. Time and cash flow are advantages. As the ex's funds start drying up, she (or he) is usually forced to switch to cheaper counsel. This can happen many times (I've seen eight as a record).

All this makes fighting expensive for the party who can afford it less! It's expensive for whichever party I am advising in the divorce as well, but this increases the odds of an advantageous settlement and avoids that lengthy, costly trial (which can cost $100,000 per week).

Strong Body and Mind, Strong Litigator

Divorces for most are negative death spirals. I've recommended many clients take this opportunity instead to perform a total hard reset. This includes adopting a clean diet, exercising, cutting out all "downers" such as alcohol and marijuana, and developing a total-control mindset including effective emotional self-regulation. Mood and energy are crucial. Successful wealthy divorcees notice their energy *increasing* "post-separation." Yes, it's stressful. Yes, it's a nuisance. But steel strengthens steel. I tell all clients to focus on these key areas:

- **Chess/Strategy**: To plan moves ahead and defend from unnecessary errors.
- **Persuasive Communication**: Use of charm, language, and persuasion to shift the mindset of the spouse (or soon-to-be ex), opposing counsel, and the judge.
- **Network**: Connections with top legal counsel, top experts, and knowledge of how to work the court system.
- **Body Language**: In-person testimony, lessons on how to present well in examinations and cross-examinations, credibility, and confidence without control freakery.

Strong inner game makes for a strong litigator.

The Secret Litigation Weapon: The Right Consultant

The big secret in high- and ultra high net worth individual divorce cases is that divorcees can (and should) hire an external litigation strategist. This hiring ought to be covert, and ideally, the divorcee's own legal counsel does not necessarily know either.

This is what I tell wealthy divorcees considering a third-party "divorce management consultant." When it comes to qualifications, you want someone who is going to give you unbiased and objective feedback (duh). Friends are there for moral support, but they are God-awful for litigation strategy. Counsel has their own bias. They're busy, and they may just want to get out the door as quickly as possible. Most family lawyers also don't trade exclusively in wealthy divorce cases; in fact, this is exceedingly rare. They don't say this, of course, but it's important to understand their context.

I always recommend someone experienced in the high net worth field. If finances are the battleground, it's wise to hire someone with specific financial expertise in these cases. I, for example, do this work all the time (for both sides).

The third-party strategist can assist in developing your side of the story. They can advise on what documents to provide and when, what opposing counsel is going after, where the soft targets are, how to reply to lines of inquiry, and how to describe the business properly and highlight the risks (without seeming like it is intentional).

The Best Offer Failed? Try This Next

So, the Best Offer from Chapter 5 failed, and now we're in litigation. What now? Here are methods I have found effective for my clients over the years, some of which we've covered so far but are now presented in a comprehensive list format among all other available options to deploy during litigation. This is how I explain each play to my clients:

1. **Hard Cut-Off**
   o Cut support payments to $0.
   o Cancel credit and bank cards.
   o No access to funds at all.
   o This is a difficult strategy to pull off in today's legal environment. It'll play as abusive to a judge (which divorcees want to mitigate if possible).

2. Soft Bleed-Out
- Substantially reduce payments to spouse—base it on something low but arguable.
- Cancel credit cards and bank cards.
- Run up legal fees for the other party by arguing anything and everything officially.
- Send numerous letters and motions.

3. Data Dumping
- Give relevant financial information at the last minute in a non-searchable PDF.
- Give no context for any documents; just dump hundreds or thousands of pages of detail at the last moment.
- Make the opposition lawyer scramble, make broad assumptions, and get key points wrong, self-immolating their own credibility.

4. Chasing Tails
- Give incomplete information.
- Say you gave everything.
- Wait a reasonable period of time.
- Give more information (still incomplete).
- Say you gave everything.
- Force them into a motion to obtain more information. Argue it's too much information, that they have everything they need.
- Give more information (still incomplete).
- End result is her counsel and expert are constantly going in and out of the file, getting confused about what's been asked for and received, running up costs substantially in the meantime.

5. Stone Wall
- Give some information.
- Argue that what you've given is reasonable.
- Argue what they're asking for is excessive.
- Force them into a motion to obtain more information.

○ If you lose, provide the information but no context. Provide as little information as possible and nothing more.

○ Argue you've given everything.

○ Force into more motions until they give up and make assumptions.

6. **Smoke Screen**

○ Have a bunch of companies—some with operations, some holding companies.

○ Have all the companies borrow funds from each other all the time.

○ Pay company debts personally and run up due to shareholder balance.

○ Have ever changing needs of each company—ideally with all of them owing money to several other organizations at a given moment.

○ Take draws from companies as shareholder loans.

○ Don't apply against due to shareholder balance.

○ Keep doing this.

○ Makes life overwhelmingly confusing to opposing counsel and experts as they need to "unwind" this giant mess.

7. **Scuttling**

○ Tank the business.

○ Blame divorce and related consequences.

○ Set up business in another jurisdiction or have someone else do it for you.

8. **Business and Personal Expense Co-Mingling**

○ Pay for personal stuff in the business.

○ Pay for business stuff personally.

○ Make it a long list of things to adjust for and maybe/maybe not catch.

○ Book personal trips but ensure you're meeting with some client there and document it as the reason for the trip.

9. **In and Out Personal Loans**

○ Loan money to the company.

○ Company repays some.

    o   Loan more money.

    o   Company repays ALL and MORE.

    o   Then loan money back to the company.

10. Loan the Company Cash before Separation

    o   Take draws against "Due to Shareholder Balance" post-separation.

    o   Argue it's not income, it's just a repayment of debt.

11. Lower That Number

    o   Planned expansion.

    o   Business needs cash flow.

    o   Capital Expenditures.

    o   Whatever else that sucks up Cash Flow in the Business.

    o   Planned Capital/Geographic Expansion.

    o   Planned Line of Business Expansion.

    o   Ongoing Commitments.

12. Low Open Market Price-Seeking

    o   Solicit below-market value offers on your business.

    o   Use as evidence that business is worth less than what experts are saying.

13. Shaking the Box

    o   Change your business model. Used to be service-only? Get into manufacturing where relevant. Manufacturing business? Start a consulting division.

    o   Change Industries.

    o   Make it hard to pin down everything you're doing and assign a hard value to it.

14. Minority Stakes as Loans

    o   Purchase some minority stakes in other private businesses.

    o   Call them loans.

    o   Tell counsel you're not sure about repayment since the company you "lent" money to is in financial trouble.

15. Conversion to Assets

    o   Buy capital assets to use in the business.

    o   Buy private investments in the business (call them loans).

- ○ Deplete cash flow by investing in things (that may or may not pay off later).

16. Red Herrings
- ○ Scatter a bunch of personal seeming expenses run through the business in a variety of accounts. Your bookkeeper misclassified these expenses and actually called them the wrong things.
- ○ Oops, your bookkeeper recorded these wrong. It reads $10,000 to JW Marriott Hotels but it's actually $10,000 to Just In Time Inventory (a legitimate supplier).
- ○ Provide evidence that the amounts are correct and they are legitimate business expenses.

17. The Fake Because
- ○ Give reasons for the way things are that are (kind of) true but paint things the way you want it to be.
- ○ Yes, revenues are up—but that's because COVID-19 ended and people are spending more. It's a one-time increase; it will decline surely enough.

18. The Hansel and Gretel
- ○ Leave a trail of unusual expenses going away from a major target.
- ○ Let's say you don't want one specific company really looked at.
- ○ Create a giant mess in the other with some of the before mentioned tactics.
- ○ Tell opposing counsel or the expert that the other company is really simple—"just does XYZ"—but the company they're looking at is the major operating entity.

19. Gold-Keepers
- ○ Have your business enterprises held by Gold-Keepers (Remember Divorce Accounting 101 in Chapter 2? That's what these experts are hired to do.)
- ○ Own ten businesses, but really only one (if necessary) in your own name.

- o Other businesses loan money to your one operating company at high interest rates (also known as profit-stripping).
- o Your one company is barely profitable and worth very little as a result—but your other companies are valuable (and off-book).

20. The *L'etat c'est Moi*

- o "I am the Business, the Business is Me."
- o Overemphasize the PERSONAL GOODWILL in the business.
- o "Really, all these customers come because of personal relationships I've developed over the years. If I'm gone, they'll all just leave."
- o This is HIGHLY effective at tanking a business valuation for this reason—often results in a push from "Income-Based" to "Asset-Based," which will work in your favor.

21. Hot/Cold

- o Be kind and charming.
- o Then be combative.
- o Flip between the two—hot and cold. Make it completely at random. Or be really happy providing them with the information you DON'T want to give, and a huge pain on information you DO want to give (only works if a pattern of randomness is established in advance).

This is by no means an exhaustive list, but it encompasses many of the strategies that can be deployed going through litigation. They can absolutely be combined for maximum effectiveness. I always tell clients to ensure they use them credibly (or at least passably credibly).

It is perfectly OK for opposing counsel and experts to know that you are playing these games (just not the mind games of Chapter 7, as that backfires). The trick here in responding to a rejected Best Offer is to hit a sweet spot where the other party doesn't have evidence to levy actions into an adverse decision.

Exercise extreme caution with some of these tactics while understanding that others are relatively low risk. For example, the Soft Bleed-Out is a great way to put an ex in a corner over time and force them to want all this to end, accepting a deal that they wouldn't have at the start.

The Psychology of Discovery

A primary issue in divorce is that the trust in the relationship is GONE. Any and all bluffs will be called. I tell my clients this: You will be asked for bank statements, credit card statements, personal and corporate tax returns, general ledgers, even specific invoices. Be prepared—but . . .

DRAG.

THIS.

PROCESS.

OUT.

I want the opposing expert and counsel to be constantly going in and out of the file. It's incredibly frustrating to start work, then stop due to a lack of information, then start again, then

stop again. So I advise giving documents towards the end of deadlines—and only giving *most* of what's asked. I'll suggest my clients make "errors" or "oversights" (not too blatantly) and "forget" issues already discussed.

> Opposing Counsel: "You forgot to give me X."
> My Client: "No, I didn't, you've been provided with EVERYTHING."
> Opposing Counsel: "I reviewed everything again and you forgot X."
> My Client: "Oh—let me see if I have that. Maybe I don't have it and that's why. I'll need to check my records but I'm tied up with meetings today and tomorrow."
> <Wait a couple days.>
> My Client: "I'm so sorry for the delay—I completely forgot. Please see attached."

Keep in mind—these delays need to be plausible. Don't push it too far; we want it to be noticeable, not provable.

The intended outcome is to "punch down" any financial assessments made during the discovery stage of litigation where all documents are presented by both sides to one another to the greatest extent possible. The primary role of income assessments, business valuations, and forensics in general in these cases is to have an independent and (ideally) unbiased expert in common with respect to income for the purposes of alimony and child support as well as the business' fair

market value at the time of separation for the division of property. A bad income assessment and valuation can be a death blow to the ability to operate successfully going forward. It's important to recognize this as a significant risk to the business and liquidity, as many business owners already face severe liquidity crunches going through divorce.

Why? Let's break this down with an example. Let's say a husband and wife own a house (bought together) worth $2 million dollars. There's a mortgage outstanding of $1 million. There aren't any other material assets or liabilities. The wife doesn't earn income. The man, being the breadwinner that he is, has a successful enterprise earning $500,000 per annum in profit. Let's just say it's a service business to keep things simple. He doesn't really have any available means of debt financing at present. But his ex has hired a business valuator. That expert has calculated a fair market value of the business of $5 million dollars. The husband can sell his business in reality at a full market value of $3,000,000. On paper, the ex is worth $500,000 (her half share of the house). But he's worth $5,500,000 (half share of house plus the business). And so he now owes her $2,500,000. So he gives her the house *and* still owes her $2,000,000. Congratulations! The man gets to sell part of his business and is now a minority shareholder in his own company.

This outcome is avoidable. The shrewd negotiator in a divorce understands discovery and the forensic duties that go into hunting down any and all cash and assets.

First and foremost, we the experts conducting these forensics examinations are looking for any and all evidence of **cash** and **unreported**

sales. Women almost always raise this as an issue. If we don't find it but still think it's there, we may try to back into sales amounts via

lifestyle analysis. Meaning we're going to tally up personal expenditures in a year—and use

that as a barometer of what the real income is. We'll also look at ratios of common expenses to sales and compare it to industry averages. If this shows an anomaly (e.g., cost of sales is way higher as a percentage of revenue than industry averages), prepare to be hammered on this.

Next are **assets**, which can be hidden in a number of ways:

- Bank accounts (domestic or foreign)
- Companies
- Cryptocurrency (Forensics generally doesn't know how to deal with this yet)
- Real property
- High value convertible assets (i.e. Rolexes, jewelry, art)

Company spin-offs are a concern as well. A common way people try to hide income or assets is to "spin off" a section of their business as a related party (family member, close friend, gold-keeper). You will already be familiar with this from Chapter 2.

Now, if the ex has filed for divorce already, trying the spin-off strategy now is the World's Worst Decision. Someone like me will figure this out most, if not all of the time. The financials will show it—the man and his wife split and suddenly revenue cuts in half for no reason? I'll just run company searches on all close associates.

But if the high net worth individual is "pre-planning" according to Chapter 2, chances are I won't find those spin-off companies. But this is a five-year horizon strategy (and don't touch the money that goes to the new entity). If the divorcee can argue the sale was legitimate, they may be fine. If they can't (i.e., it's obviously to get around paying support), they will have major issues.

A better way (more legal) to do this is to also own the company spin-off. In fact, high net worth individuals may own several company spin-offs. They don't manage the day-to-day operations of the spin-offs—and they also keep the money in these new entities to every extent possible. They might form ten companies (this may seem like a lot, but I've seen more) and run all manner of transactions between the new entities and the original operating company.

What they're doing is creating a giant confusing mess of perfectly legitimate companies where

They can then argue that:

1. They don't have hands-on management of the new entities and therefore the income from these companies is not really accessible . . .
2. . . . because the income is inaccessible, it shouldn't be included in their "income."

To close out this discovery section, know that the judiciary is overburdened with cases. NO judge wants to unravel this mess, and the cost of an expert doing so and being able to articulate it clearly in court to a judge will likely be prohibitively high.

The Expert Interviewing of Experts

Forensic expert witnesses called in during litigation are supposed to be unbiased. But in reality, many *are* biased, and if the opposing party has hired them, they will be extremely biased. That won't necessarily be blatant. That's too risky.

Experts are looking for clues, and we "play it cool" while we snoop. At a high level, we're looking for anomalies such as personal expenses run through the business, sudden changes in revenue and expense balances, and hidden assets. We start with low-hanging fruit and work our way up the tree until satisfied.

The divorcee's job when being interviewed by an expert is to lead this person where they, the divorcee, want the conversation to go, not where the expert wants it.

Anything said to any expert can and will be used against the person interviewed. Therefore, I tell my clients exactly this: You need to "prime" the expert up front and quickly. I have my clients take the opportunity to explain a few things at the start. For example, I'll tell them to say:

1. Your business was getting worse (income falling, or if not NEW RISK in the market) leading up to separation. Hang your hat on something that is objectively true.
   o Lost some big clients?
   o New entrants to market?
   o Price competitiveness?
   o Cost increases and supply chain issues?
   o Whatever out of this "fits"—USE IT!
2. Post Separation—guess what? Your business has continued getting worse.
   o The separation has been extremely hard.
   o Depression.
   o Inability to focus.
   o Putting out fires.
   o Anything under point 1. if it applies too.

I call this "priming for the divorce dive" so anything otherwise interpreted as an anomaly now makes sense, according to my client's story. After all, business performance has a "tendency" to get worse post-separation. Sometimes, it's perfectly legitimate—for any of the above noted reasons. Sometimes, it's total bullshit; the person is hiding income or deferring invoicing for sales made until later. So I want my clients to give the interviewing expert a plausible reason for why the business has tanked post-separation.

A Few Words on Recording Conversations

Now, I'd actually recommend recording any phone calls or meetings with experts. Check local jurisdictions on rules for recording conversations. In some places, it is fine if *one* person knows the conversation is being recorded. In others, both parties need to know. If it's both, or to play on the safe side, caution the other party up front that the conversation will be recorded. If anything, they'll be terrified—and will be much more "by the book" on what is said versus willfully incorrectly interpreting a statement. Clients who do this succeed, which means keeping the expert's head down, staring at the ground, for all that low-hanging fruit that's already fallen. No climbing up any trees for the "ripe" and "juicy" bits.

Deposition Strategy and Tactics

Depositions (or examinations for discovery) is the first real test divorcees face in litigation. The primary objective is to put facts on the formal record. Opposing counsel will ask a series of questions. They know the answers usually, the interviewee knows the answers, but they have to play along. Put differently, opposing counsel is assessing whether they want to take this thing to trial. Thus, failing depositions and appearing not credible is an enormous problem to come back from.

How to Attend a Deposition, Examination, or Informal Interview

Understand what the final product of a deposition is: a wearyingly long transcript of questions and responses, black and white, on paper, with all the *ums, hmms, uh-huhs, yeps*, etc. all left in. So I tell my clients to choose their words carefully. Long pauses, however, do not show up. It is acceptable to take as much time as needed to verbalize every response.

What's Important, What Isn't Important

At a deposition, the divorcee's objective is to show up, answer questions, and appear as credible as possible. Does this mean they need to know everything? No. Does this mean they have to tell the whole truth and nothing but the truth? Also no. By now, you understand the importance of planning. You or your client will need to craft a story, which is as realistic as possible, but benefits you (or them). And this needs to be done well in advance of deposition, and practice. And stay ON SCRIPT—the purpose of storytelling in Chapter 7 is to prepare for this.

What We Are Looking For

Opposing counsel is looking for two things.

1. Catch the interviewee in a lie.
2. Make them disclose more information than they should.

Remember that depositions are transcripts on the record. Deposition traps are REAL. If the divorcee says one thing at the deposition and changes their story at trial, they will absolutely be called out for this.

Tactics to Gain Information

Lawyers utilize all manner of psychological tricks to obtain more disclosure and gain valuable information. They have ideas well in advance of deposition and in many cases will already know where to start probing lines of inquiry.

I tell my clients to, at the beginning of a deposition, expect easy questions and calm opposing counsel. Easy Yes or No. Correct or Incorrect. Short answer. *What day were you married? When did you separate? How many kids do you have?* These lull the interviewee into automatic responses. Then the games begin. Here's what they are, how they're played, and what I tell my clients to do or say in response:

1. **Loaded Questions**: When did you stop abusing your wife?
2. **Two Questions in One** (usually with opposing answers): Is it true that you withheld money from your ex-wife and committed financial abuse?
   - If you don't like the question or framing—tell them you don't understand it and ask to rephrase it.
3. **The Wind Up**: Remember, depositions are a black and white document. Pauses and tone of voice are NOT recorded.

- OC will often attempt to wind you up. Start peppering with questions, cutting you off mid sentence, and making accusations. NONE of this matters. You must stay calm, and focused.
- They will accuse you of spinning the truth, not answering the question, lying, stealing, and fraud. NONE of this matters. Stay Calm and Focused.
- Being combative reads poorly. Don't spout off. Stay 100% professional at all times.

4. **You Don't Know What They Know**: Watch for questions about things that are true. You'll be caught off guard that they know this. Answer honestly, but mitigate the damage (unless this is clearly a fishing question).

5. **Fishing Questions**: Wild leaps of logic to see what comes up. Is it true you have a bank account in the Cayman Islands? (No, you have one in Barbados!)
   - Just say NO. Don't elaborate.

6. **Open-Ended Questions**: Answer as succinctly as possible. Do NOT give information away.

7. **Forced Closed-Ended Questions**: They will specifically ask you to respond Yes or No. And guess what, both responses are bad. Explain that you have to give a longer response because it isn't a yes or no question.

8. **Accusations**. It's OK to call these out, e.g., "That accusation is unwarranted, I don't appreciate your tone."

9. **Dramatic Body Language**. The intent is to increase the tension in the room.
   - Expect pointing at you; expect eye rolling. Call it out, e.g., "I don't appreciate you rolling your eyes every time I answer a question. You thrusting your fingers at me is upsetting and not necessary."

I remind my clients of this final point: The judge reads everything. Anything said, they also will use against you.

Counter Tactics at Deposition

The shrewd interviewee has three simple goals to accomplish at deposition. Here's how I explain them to my clients:

1. Stick to the script and maintain the frame and story you've outlined (but don't take notes to deposition). If you go off script, update your notes for later (e.g., at trial)
2. Stay calm and credible.
3. Limit bad information and accentuate all the information that's good to your case.

Shutting Down Lines of Inquiry

Having good counsel is important. Problem questions must be shut down quickly. Again, it is acceptable to PAUSE before answering any questions. This gives counsel a chance to interject about the relevance of a question or whether their client may either answer or not. This also helps drag out the time. I want my clients' lawyers to interject as many times as possible (within reason) and burn time with the two lawyers arguing whether it's an appropriate question or not.

If the question must be answered, an easy out (to be deployed only as necessary is, "I don't recall that at the moment." This shuts it down and also allows for introducing new evidence about what's been asked about, later. After deposition. Without being stuck with whatever is being asked.

Another tactic to shut things down is to muddy the waters. Provide incoherent responses that are at times yes, at times no, at times responding to the question, at times responding to another question. This one is hard to pull off—if opposing counsel is competent, they'll suspect something's up and will climb back up the tree where there appears to be fruit—the good stuff.

Now, some lawyers like to go HARD in inquiry, becoming animated and combative—think

Judge Judy. This type of examination or inquiry is the easiest to defeat. I tell my clients this: Take a deep breath. Smile inside. Know you'll win out if you keep composure and answer with (your version of)

the truth. Keep a poker pace. Stay on message. Remain calm. Opposing counsel notices this, perceives credibility, and realizes a victory at trial is not guaranteed.

That said, other attorneys and experts (like me) are less obvious and more sinister in terms of style during a deposition, examination, or interview. Here are two tactics I use heavily during litigation when I'm called in to interview someone:

1. **Sprezzatura**
2. **Columbo'ing**

Sprezzatura is known in the fashion world; it's akin to a relaxed "I don't care" look while actually caring about your look. The key is I don't *seem* to care. I use this almost all the time—I'm relaxed, open, even warm to people I'm investigating. If it's off-record, I'll tell the odd joke. I address by first name and ask loose, open-ended questions, I'll then ask loose, open-ended questions about their responses. It's informal-seeming. I'll even go so far as to appear to not be paying attention at certain points of the interview. I want the interviewee to think I'm just going through the motions. Really? I'm paying close attention to what they want to talk about and where they're trying to lead me so I then know where "all the bodies are buried" (these are whatever they choose to not discuss).

To an outside observer, an interview with me will look a lot more like an interview with *Success* or *Forbes* than a hard-hitting deposition. This is intentional; I want people inclined to shut down, to open up. I use this, I ask probing questions but never give away that I'm on to something. My objective is to keep the other party talking about relevant details, then use this evidence later in any way possible. The more information I have, the better.

My second strategy—the **Columbo**—comes towards the end of the interview. It's been on the classic TV show *Columbo* about a detective who lulled suspects into condemning themselves without realizing that's what he was up to. So for example, my final question is always, "Oh, wait . . . just one more thing," like Columbo might ask. By that point, I've taken the interviewee on what was (sometimes) an hours-long interview about their business, personal life, and finances.

There's always one thing I want to ask at the end. Maybe I have some information they don't know I have. Let's say I've found records of an offshore bank account. The ex-husband thought it secret and doesn't know his ex found a copy of a statement rummaging around his office.

"Oh, wait . . . just one more thing. Is this a copy of your bank account statement in the Cayman Islands?"

"Yes."

CHAPTER 9

LEGAL MONEY LAUNDERING?

The wealthy and wise who plan their finances with a non-zero chance of divorce understand "legal money laundering" better than many forensic accounts ever will. No, it's not technically money laundering. Yes, we've touched on aspects of this so far. And yes, it is all highly legal. And yet no, that doesn't mean all will agree—especially if the eventual divorcee makes a target of himself.

When I was on safari in South Africa, I started asking the driver questions that I likely shouldn't have, sitting in an open-air Land Rover with a giant elephant rifle in front of me. It was not for elephants.

I spotted a lion a few yards away resting behind a bush so I said, "What's stopping that lion from jumping in here?"

"Perception," the driver, a local who seemed utterly unphased, said.

"OK, but how many people would that lion kill if he decided he was hungry and we looked tasty?"

"Everyone."

"But what about the gun? Wouldn't that play some role here?"

"Not really. Maybe a couple of us will survive."

"Oh."

The gun, like seatbelts on an airplane, was mostly decorative. Survival came down to the lion's perception of the Land Rover. See, when a lion looks at a truck, it perceives all of us and the truck as one giant animal. It doesn't perceive the truck and people separately and therefore views jumping into the truck as too high a risk. It's when the people *leave* the truck that they risk getting eaten.

Legal money laundering in this context is exactly the same. When nothing changes and everyone stays calm, the lion (people like me) have challenges differentiating between truck and human, or legitimate complex business activities from illegitimate (and yet still entirely legal in some jurisdictions, as I've described previously). It's when the dumb rich (usually men) get served the paper, panic, and jump out of the truck that the lion now has targets to chase.

This is lion psychology. Now, lions are different, and what most normal sane people would view as stressful, lions view as fun and games. And so "boring" and "more of the same" are ideal perceptions for survival for the high net worth who divorce. Interesting, novel, and challenging are very bad. Sudden changes around the time of separation equal lion food.

Safe inside the Truck

People like me perform financial analytics to see if anyone gets out of the truck. Here's how to stay *in* the truck.

The first thing needed is Microsoft Excel. It's best to set up all the financial statements similarly and be able to see multiple years (ideally five or more) all together to get a sense of what's happening with the business historically. This is great practice for any investment being considered into a business, as an aside. The human brain is not designed to flip through several pages of documents and numbers and see trends. By compiling information in one spot, the wealthy individual can see what an expert will see and be able to anticipate where the questions will be focused before speaking with them.

Year-Over-Year Changes

One useful technique is to set "expectations" of what account balances should be based on given factors. Expense accounts can be divided into:

1. **Variable** - fluctuations are expected somewhat in line with revenue
2. **Fixed** - generally expect an inflationary increase (like rent expense)
3. **Mixed** - slot 50 percent into fixed and 50 percent into variable and project this balance Then compare these expectations to the actual financials. What's different and why? Use these questions to focus the scope of the engagement. If cost of sales is expected to increase by 10 percent with revenue but it increases by 50 percent, information is missing. It's important to hone in on this to figure out what is really happening.

Lines of inquiry should be a funnel:

- **Broad questions** - Why did the price of this input increase?
- **Narrow questions** - Request to see a list of invoices from a specific supplier.
- **Fine detail** - Use this if necessary, as it involves a deep dive into "supporting evidence" to establish a baseline.

For example, if someone owned a pancake and waffle mix company, the expectation is that the input (ingredients to blend) cost will increase proportionately with revenue. If these costs skyrocket after a certain event, what's going on? Potential answers include:

- The prices of the inputs rose dramatically due to inflation.
- The blend was changed to a more premium product.

To verify, request invoices from before and after the event to see if prices have increased and/or the mix has changed. If this doesn't fully explain the cost increase, a deep dive is needed. Go through invoices of the inputs and start comparing the quantity of input to sales volumes.

For example, if they historically ordered 100kg of input and sold 95kg of pancake mix (some inventory loss is expected), but now they order 100kg of input and only sell 50kg of pancake mix, this could indicate hidden income. This provides reason to go on a "fishing expedition" for other information.

Note that an opposing expert is not going to reveal this type of finding over the phone or in person. They won't make an allegation directly. They will just ask questions and gather information. The full findings will only be shared when their report is served prior to trial.

Common Ratios Analyzed

As alluded to previously, normalizing financial statements (specifically income/profit and loss statements) against revenue is useful. This means not only tracking the real dollar value, but looking at expense balances expressed as a percentage of revenue. This is known as "common-sizing." Often, charting these on a graph is helpful, especially if nothing obvious stands out from the numbers alone. Sometimes a visual depiction will reveal insights the raw data does not.

When dealing with balance sheet issues (assets and liabilities), the most common ratios are:

- Debt to equity ratio
- Quick or current ratio
- Liquidity ratios

It's also useful to compare "common-size" expenses to revenue ratios against industry averages for same/similar businesses operating in geographically similar territories.

Where Issues Are Often Found

These are some common accounts to look at first for potential irregularities:

- **Travel** - family trips
- **Meals/entertainment** - family dining, solo coffees, etc.
- **Advertising/promotion** - tickets to events, golfing, liquor store/ wine purchases, prepaid visa cards, high ticket luxury goods
- **Automobile expenses** - assigning a percentage to personal use based on mileage
- **Salary/wages** - relatives or friends on payroll

- **Subcontractors** - again, relatives or friends
- **Marketing** - a common "dumping ground" for fun expenses
- **Office expenses/computers** - personal items like home electronics
- **Utilities** - some people run household utilities through their businesses
- **Telephone** - family smartphone plans
- **Repairs and maintenance or leasehold improvements** - the office doesn't look recently renovated, so what was?

The Divorce Dive

The parties separate, and suddenly the business just loses clients and bleeds cash. This often supports the assertion that income or business valuation is being intentionally understated.

Normalizing Adjustments

Normalizing adjustments are a staple of business valuations. The purpose is to present the financial statements as they would be when a third party purchases the business. In other words, it calculates the business' value to the purchaser.

This is important because for most operating businesses, the fair market value is calculated utilizing some version of income, usually called "maintainable earnings," "maintainable cash flow," or something similar. A multiple is applied to this maintainable income to calculate the total entity value. The multiple could be 2X earnings, 10X earnings, etc. It depends on the specific business.

"Maintainable" is a key concept. It refers to how much earnings/cash flow/income is reasonably maintainable going forward. There is incentive to reduce this maintainable amount as much as possible. Here are some legitimate ways to do this:

1. Argue the owner's salary is below market value. For example, if they pay themselves $100,000 per year, but a CEO/President salary is typically $175,000.

2. Argue it would take two people to replace the owner, like a CEO and CMO, because they've been working 90 hour weeks.
3. Point out any one-time only revenues. For example, if they were hired to provide branded t-shirts for a major company's 100th anniversary and the revenue was $500,000, argue this won't continue in the future and should be backed out.
4. Note a permanent increase in expense prices. If an important input has recently increased in cost by 20 percent, factor this into the model.

These examples depend on the specific business and situation, which is why hiring a strategist in advance to dig through everything and find these pressure points is recommended. Adjusting the maintainable earnings amount downwards by $200,000 could save hundreds of thousands of dollars or more in a separation.

Red Flag Indicators

The biggest red flag is always a lifestyle that far exceeds declared income. For example, if someone is paying a million-dollar mortgage, has luxury vehicles, sends kids to private school, but claims to make $25,000 per year, further investigation is warranted.

Similarly, stories from the other party about the marriage can reveal potential issues, such as:

1. No matter where he went, he always traveled with a few thousand dollars in cash
2. He recently bought expensive watches with unknown funds
3. He would always buy expensive things and pay cash
4. If there's an "online business," consider cryptocurrency
5. He talked about cryptocurrency a lot and was obsessed with his phone
6. Recurring trips to tax havens
7. A safe in the house

Cryptocurrency is an interesting new area that is difficult to track down. Buying crypto from exchanges leaves a paper trail via bank statements that provides reason to subpoena records.

Dates of Interest as Trigger Points of Inquiry

Often, hiding income or assets starts after being served with divorce papers. Requesting financial information for the three years prior to separation serves as a baseline to spot anomalies that pop up after the split.

This assumes there hasn't been pre-planning for divorce all along, which is much harder to catch. If income was already being hidden or funds siphoned off in the years leading up to divorce, it won't stand out as much after the split because it's already "baked in." The baseline is wrong.

If divorce was planned all along, the other party shouldn't catch wind of it. The bias of the system works in favor here, with most divorces being initiated by women. Lawyers and experts will tend to believe the man was surprised and didn't pre-plan.

One potential "tell" of pre-planning is a combination of financial sophistication, narcissistic traits, and limited ethical boundaries. If the spouse has been told about many creative ways people have been screwed over in business deals or how taxes are avoided or dodged, this information will likely be passed on to their lawyer. The less the spouse knows about the "how" of success, the better.

Pattern Recognition and Identifying Oddities

Fraudsters tend to only be slightly creative. Once they find a system that works, it gets repeated, creating patterns that stick out when reviewing bank accounts or general ledgers. This also makes it easy to protect what's really going on here.

For example, consider an oil and gas industry parts manufacturing company. The intent is to have a friend invoice monthly for services they aren't providing, to shelter cash in a dummy corporation. The friend invoices $10,000 per month. This often happens with services like "management consulting," "IT consulting," etc.

Looking at this, it would be odd for a manufacturing company to hire a "management consultant" for $10,000 per month with no clear increase in profitability. What is this consultant doing exactly? This is just one example of many potential patterns to watch for.

The Finer Details

It's common knowledge that operating a business comes with perks, like writing off some personal expenses. Some are obvious, like taking the family on a vacation to Hawaii and writing it off. These are quick to discover.

The analysis can stop there or continue into finer details if necessary. At a certain point, it becomes pure grunt work to deploy when the story being told doesn't match the reality seen.

This involves going through every bank statement (personal and corporate) to figure out the source of all deposits. Many deposits of unknown origin will be found, prompting questions and requests for backup evidence like invoices. The same process is applied to expenses, including personal and corporate credit cards.

The end result is knowing what's being deposited, where, and why, as well as where cash is flowing out. Having many deposits or expenses with no explanation is a big red flag.

Corporate Structures and Following the Money

When someone owns multiple businesses, especially if funds are exchanged between them, using flow charts to "follow the money" can be effective. This is especially useful with judges who are busy and don't want to do a deep forensic dive to understand a case.

Mapping out cash flows can highlight hidden income or assets that someone is trying to mask via a "smoke screen" or "ring around the rosey" scheme of sending money back and forth between entities to create confusion.

Due diligence searches are also effective for uncovering hidden income or assets. If significant questions remain after analysis, title searches on property and corporate searches on ownership/directorship should be performed for:

1. The business owner's name
2. The business(es) itself
3. Close friends/business associates' names
4. Family members' names

Backing into Income When All Else Fails

As a last resort, attempting to "back into" income by analyzing expenses from the ground up can be done. This means completely ignoring stated income and focusing on expenditures.

For example:

- Mortgage payments of $4,000 per month = $48,000 per year
- Groceries of $1,000 per month = $12,000 per year
- Vacations of $10,000 per year
- Car expenses of $20,000 per year
- Entertainment/clothes/other of $20,000 per year
- Miscellaneous household expenses of $20,000 per year

Adding these up shows $130,000 per year is required on an after-tax basis to fund this lifestyle. Grossed up to account for income taxes, the income is probably around $175,000 per year minimum (assuming the above are not debt/investment financed). This is an easy, effective way to establish a minimum income level for a business owner, especially when there have been attempts to obfuscate their real income.

Staying in the truck requires discipline. Only those who survive have it.

CHAPTER 10

WHAT HAPPENS AT TRIAL STAYS IN THE PUBLIC RECORD

Trial preparation is critically important and completely overlooked in the divorce industry. The stakes of a trial are extremely high. Testimony at trial is life-changing. There are no take-backs; there are no second chances. Access to children—and extreme wealth consequences—hang on one or a few days of testifying and withstanding the brutality of cross-examination. And the typical trial preparation meeting between attorney and client is one or perhaps two hours—not so for the wealthy who remain so following their divorce. And yet most, even those with sizable income and considerable assets, botch trial prep. Millions of dollars. Children in limbo. One hour of preparation. This is bad. How bad? I will tell you.

Meet Joseph. Joseph had the unfortunate experience of being on the other side of my litigation consulting business, meaning that my role was to run his wife's case from behind the scenes, leading all the way up to a trial, where Joseph did not fare well.

Joseph at the time was an established entrepreneur with several business interests and a substantial annual income. He was a hundred-million-dollar man. At no surprise to anyone, when his ex-wife filed for divorce, all of the businesses began to fail.

"I'm broke!" were his words.

There were allegations of other wrongdoing throughout the marriage; the details are unimportant, and there was no real evidence that would substantiate them. And so his ex-wife would say he was an abusive, narcissistic sociopath, but when asked for evidence to support any of this, her claims boiled down to "Well, he was, like, super mean . . . sometimes." I'm sure Joseph probably was. On a long enough time frame, men and women alike tend to say or do mean things.

We reached trial with Broke Joseph and his extensive and expensive legal team showing up ready for him. Joseph's direct testimony (with his attorney asking the questions) was fine. No major errors, boring, intelligent.

Yet men, and especially successful men, have an unfortunate trait where their estimation of their "logic" and "legal mind" stands head-and-shoulders above reality. *They are bad at this stuff.* And so cross-examination brought fireworks.

When designing questions against rich men, my personal experience tells me that front-loading cross examination with highly emotionally charged topics bears a lot of fruit for my clients (in these cases, their ex-wives). So I wanted Joseph to be highly emotional and combative. In boxing terms, this is forcing an orthodox fighter to southpaw. Logic is gone; emotions take over.

All the initial cross examination questions were tailored to put Joseph into this highly emotional state. This is where making accusations of abuse, then going into detail about each instance cited by his ex-wife became valuable.

"Isn't it correct that you're an abusive person and on such and such date you verbally assaulted my client and said [insert bad things here]?"

"Do you think as a successful man that you can do anything and that's why over the course of the marriage you believed it was acceptable to be an abusive husband?"

Enough of these questions in a row, and Joseph became highly agitated and combative, and started calling his ex-wife all kinds of names—and even began doing this to her lawyer.

What the judge saw was this: Joseph denied the allegations of abuse while being directly (and inappropriately) abusive sitting there on the stand with his ex-wife *and* her attorney. Broke Joseph's credibility evaporated.

After this, we got into the financial details of Joseph's businesses where this pattern continued. Joseph would double-down, then double-down again on some of the provably false claims he had made about his business affairs. It likely didn't help that he was sporting a Rolex during trial. Yes, we pointed this out.

And so it was obvious to all that *I'm broke!* was *not* true when Joseph uttered those words during trial. Afterwards, his was a self-fulfilling prophecy. Largely due to his cross-examination performance, the judge found Joseph to be *incredible*. Meaning, not credible. His expert's evidence on the business valuations and his income was largely ignored. His ex-wife's expert's opinion on these issues was accepted—despite these figures being far higher than reality and laden with issues of their own.

Trial performance is important.

What to Expect at Trial

The greater the preparation, the greater the odds of victory. The opposite is true, as was probably the case with Broke Joseph. He did not come across like someone who had given much thought to how he intended to come across during cross-examination.

To men (and women) who wish to experience a very different [outcome], I tell this:

- Expect your feelings of whether you're winning or losing to interchange frequently and freely.
- Expect that when you're done "on the stand," you'll think you've lost. If you think you've won, you've probably lost.
- Expect to be called names.
- Expect your ex to play the crying (or raging) game. Emotions will arise.

Anticipation of and response to any and all emotional discomfort at trial is key. The first line of both offense and defense is nonverbal communication. I'll explain.

Body Language Persuasion at Trial

Regarding dress code, I tell clients to wear a suit and tie (or pantsuit, for women). Appear presentable and credible. Don't overdo anything, especially not with flamboyance—don't bring the solid gold Rolex to trial, like Broke Joseph.

Take a shower, shave (goes for women, too; you'd be surprised!), and avoid wearing cologne or perfume. Wear glasses if you have them.

Now, your stature is much-dependent on the narrative. If it's helpful to appear "smaller," dress plainer and simpler. If it's helpful to appear "confident," look like a boss.

Not that matrimonial law involves a jury trial, but if you happen to be in a jury trial situation, DO NOT BRING THE LAMBO. Rent something reasonable, as jurors need to park, too, after all.

Examination-in-Chief

The sharp divorcee's objective is open-ended storytelling—big picture and introduction of evidence and narrative to support their case. They speak relatively freely, deploying evidence as necessary and avoiding all *ad hominem* attacks. Let's get into the specifics, for when the questions come and what to say back.

Cross Examination Essentials

I tell all my clients this: Your objective is to give closed-down responses while maintaining your same appearance and mannerisms as under direct examination, i.e., taking questions for your own legal counsel. Maintain guard and frame, not losing control of the narrative.

Warming up before your time in court is an absolute necessity because it is a stressful situation you're entering into. Start talking to everyone and anyone you can. Ask the court police officer as you enter the courthouse how their day is going. Spend an extra three minutes at Starbucks chatting up the barista. Call a friend on the way. Do whatever gets you chatting. You want to be chatty heading into court. Once you hit the stand, that "chattiness" will subside naturally from this baseline.

Maintaining Credibility and Persuading along the Way

Everyone gets something wrong. This is the false legal confidence I was telling you about early. The fool who is soon parted with his money believes he can slip up, doublespeak, and pretend nothing happened. No, that's not correct; any error molehills will be made mountains of by opposing counsel during cross-examination. This is inevitable. They will take a small error and try to rattle the witness by making that one issue speak for all others.

"You said X before, and now you're saying Y. How can we trust ANYTHING you say?"

Patience. This demands patience. I ask my clients this: What's more important? Being right about one thing, or maintaining credibility over everything? They get the idea: Do NOT DOUBLE DOWN. If you're caught, you're caught.

"You're right—my recollection was incomplete when I said that. My apologies; you're right."

Understand that lawyers ask intentionally confusing questions during cross-examinations with the intent to create the appearance of lying. For example, compound questions. This is where the divorcee will be asked two questions (one being an easy yes or no, the other being a nuanced

question) in the hope that the examined accepts the premise and just says yes or no.

"You're a successful entrepreneur who could easily earn $500,000 per year, wouldn't you agree?"

The frame here is trying to get immediate agreement. The natural inclination is to say yes—because the examined wants to agree that they're a successful entrepreneur, and saying no won't sit well.

The best way to handle sneaky tactics such as these is not to agree but to respectfully request confirmation. Make them provide whatever evidence they are talking about before responding.

"Can you show me what you're referring to? Can I see a copy of my calendar for that date? I don't remember. That was a long time ago."

Refutation is particularly essential when those *ad hominems* come out. It's not uncommon to see an attack on all fronts in matrimonial cases. I prepare my clients for accusations about:

- The children and the relationship
- Alleged abuse
- Narcissistic behaviors
- Cheating (without evidence)
- Drug and alcohol dependency issues
- Temper issues
- Tax fraud
- Shady business deals

The examined's job is to refute these if they come up.

"I wasn't remotely abusive, and there's been no evidence to suggest that I have been. Also, my tax accountant prepares my records—I am, as far as I'm aware, completely compliant with tax law."

If the suggestion is regarding sexual violence or abuse with the ex, a signed document with this person on what is OK versus NOT OK in the bedroom is essential. Especially if operating in the BDSM realm where lines are (understandably) blurred to the average person like a judge.

On sexual and other intimate matters, it is wise to avoid being pinned to a yes or no. Not everything is black and white in life and love nor should it be. I have told clients to literally say, "Actually, replying to that with a yes or no isn't a helpful answer to the court because it doesn't tell the whole story. Judge, your honor, may I answer the question more fully?"

Lawyers will try other tactics if these don't get under their target's skin. Lawyers love pitching hypothetical questions, but the hypothetical will always lump wealthy individuals into a category where they don't want to be. They should NOT let them!

For example, the lawyer might say, "Let's say you're a successful business owner. But like anyone successful, you have a good understanding of the finances and tax and therefore know what you can get away with on your tax returns, right?"

The divorcee should respond with something like, "This hypothetical isn't really applicable. Sure, I'm modestly successful, but I hire someone to prepare my taxes and don't really know what's involved."

Lawyers may also try restating the individual's evidence but adding on their own falsehoods. For instance, they might say, "As your accountant just agreed, this expense is a personal expense and therefore this is tax evasion."

I tell my clients that they should remember that they didn't agree to tax evasion—they just admitted it was a personal expense. They should interject on these by saying something like, "I didn't agree to tax evasion. This was an expense that was personal, but my accountant used it as a business expense, it seems. I'm not a tax expert, but he must be."

Logical fallacies are a great way for the shrewd divorcee to escape uncomfortable questions and answer direct questions in a way that benefits them. These can only be used effectively on occasion, so I suggest reserving these for circumstances necessary to maintain their effectiveness.

The **Motte and Bailey fallacy** is a convenient way to sidestep a direct question where the response would sound terrible. This simply means avoiding answering a question from a weak position and reverting to a much more defensible position. A simplistic example is:

"So you cheated on your wife?"

"No, I have always been a loving and caring husband who has provided for and protected his family."

The "no" at the beginning isn't really about the cheating—it's just refuting the premise of the question. The individual hasn't actually answered the question here, but it sounds like they have.

The Kettle Fallacy, a creation of Sigmund Freud, is based on the premise that an individual has borrowed a kettle and returned it to the owner broken. In response, they provide three simultaneous defenses:

- It was broken when they got it.
- They returned it undamaged; the owner must have broken it later.
- They never borrowed it in the first place.

It's notable that none of these arguments are remotely consistent, and that's the point. By providing three incoherent defenses, chances are one of them is right, and therefore the individual is correct in their statement. This is actually a codified legal tactic known in the US as "alternative pleading."

Poisoning the Well is something wealthy divorcees try often but rarely succeed at because the intent is so blatant. This only works if it is subversive. Calling out their ex as being lazy, a slut, a bitch, or anything derogatory will only make the accuser out as the narcissistic, egomaniacal, abusive lunatic their ex will have characterized them as, so they should avoid this at all costs.

Instead, poison the well with small but relevant details about actions rather than name-calling. All those times when their ex acted like a deranged lunatic? Perfect! They should recall these times in their context on the stand, focusing on how it made them feel. They shouldn't say their ex is a "bitch" because of it. They should say they "felt threatened." They should say it was "scary." Leave it there; let the rest go to imagination.

Also consider peppering the record with the correct narrative—the desired story the judge ought to believe. This can be done with open-ended questions to respond to things you haven't been asked yet. I tell my clients to bring up context that hasn't been presented. If their ex has been aggressive, acted threatening, or said she would kill them, they should squeeze this into questioning whenever possible.

For example, if the lawyer asks, "Is it true that you and Mrs. Woman had an argument on December 23rd, 2019?", the client should respond with something like, "Oh yes, I remember this well. I had come home late, and she accused me of cheating at knifepoint and said she was going to kill me. It was really scary—I wouldn't call this an argument so much as a hostage situation." Yes, this is also poisoning the well, but it can be effective sometimes.

Wealthy individuals should find little openings to expand on something that is favorable to their case. For instance, if the lawyer asks, "Is it true that your business was more successful last year than before?", they could respond with, "It was a bit more successful because we're online and COVID-19 restrictions helped an unusual amount, but this year the performance has really declined because of the divorce and the economy reopening. I don't know if we'll even be profitable this year." They're spinning something that looks good (to the lawyer) into something that looks bad.

Most everyone knows the **Straw Man Argument**. Divorcees can set up the straw man by taking an argument beyond its logical conclusion. For example, "All women suck at business" is a straw man argument because clearly, some do not suck. Another example is, "She just says I'm abusive because I have opinions and I voice them."

The typical form of a **Circular Argument** is "X is because Y, therefore Y is because X." For example, "Taking cocaine is against the law because it's wrong. I know it's wrong because it's against the law." Financial issues are a great area where one can interchange terms with specific meaning but rely on a judge to catch on reading the transcript later. For instance, "My revenues are going up, but my costs are going up, too. I have to buy more inventory which means that I'm less profitable." A quick read of this makes sense, but upon further examination, it's confusing. If revenues are up, obviously more product is needed for sales, so why does that mean profit is down? But that's the evidence, and it was accepted at the time.

Shrewd divorcees should use additional tactics to buy time, such as asking to repeat a question, asking to rephrase a question, saying they don't understand what the lawyer means, asking to pull up whatever document they're referring to, or asking them to point out what they're talking about on the document. Obviously, they should deploy these only when reasonable. They shouldn't ask to repeat the question when the lawyer asks for their full name, for example

What this really gets at is interview subversion. It's possible to frustrate opposing counsel by asking reasonable questions. This will cause them to change the game plan and invariably miss things and make mistakes. At a certain point, the judge will be looking at the clock and will be saying to opposing counsel, "Can you get to the point?" This is good because we want the judge to feel frustrated with counsel's questioning.

If only Broke Joseph knew 10 percent of this, everything would have turned out differently. But, alas, he did not. And the poor bastard was forced to liquidate everything to pay.

And I mean everything. Businesses, gone. Meaning he had to sell his businesses. All of them. Eight of them. All of them. His ex had been able to value all of his businesses for $100 million despite his insistence on paper that he was worth $0. He could have been convincing—had he not demolished his own credibility during cross-examination. So he owed her $50 million. But he had to sell everything all at once, including the businesses but also vacation homes and supercars—all for $40 million, so he still owed her $10 million.

Oh, and income gone, too. He'd been pulling $5 million per year from the business, we were able to suggest. Despite his insistence, again on paper, that the number was $0.

Child custody? Nope, not that either. The ex-wife won 100 percent custody of their four children including parental decision-making rights.

Game over. Broke Joseph had to start again from square one—at approximately fifty years of age. I don't envy him.

CHAPTER 11

HOW TO SMOKE THE OPPOSITION

C hapter 10 describes what to do during trial when the opposition is trying to smoke you (or your client). Chapter 11 is all about how to turn the tables, "smoke back," and win.

To help protect a divorcee's wealth, I've worked to build winning cases that are trial-ready before there is even a trial. Ideally, there's no trial at all, of course; but when there is, this is the blueprint for success. When trial is complete, the judge views my client as:

1. Credible.
2. Sympathetic.

. . . and my client's ex as:

1. Incredible.
2. Batshit-crazy (ideally).

In any area where there is room for doubt, the ideal outcome is the trial judge believing your or your client's version of events—far more than they do the (batshit-crazy) ex's version.

The Interplay of Logic and Emotions

There are two forces at play in persuasive communication:

1. Logic.
2. Emotion.

In my experience, thinking of logic and emotion as existing on a "spectrum" is misleading and fails to recognize just how closely related "hyper-emotional" communication and "hyper-logical" communication styles are. These two states are so closely related that they look the same; only the word-choices are different. This is important. I will explain.

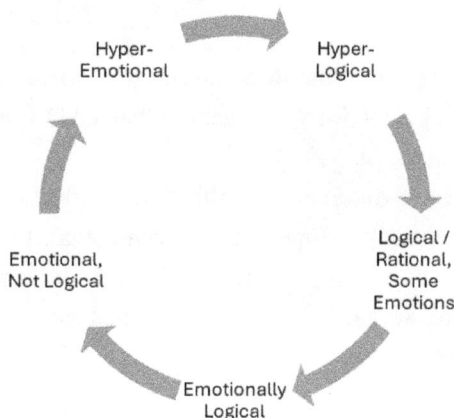

Hyper-Emotional → Hyper-Logical

Emotional, Not Logical

Logical / Rational, Some Emotions

Emotionally Logical

In normal life, most men find themselves to be either logical or mostly logical communicators. Women generally are semi-logical or entirely emotional communicators.

But this isn't normal life; it's trial. As a general rule, when preparing men for trial, my focus is installing enough **emotional self-regulation** in their psyche that they remain at the "Logical with Emotion" or "Emotionally Logical" level, this being the best Communication Level for trial—especially given the various accusations and histrionics thrown at them during cross-examination. Importantly though, I want my male client to say things that create an emotional spike for her so that by the time she is on the stand, her baseline is "Hyper-Emotional." Put differently, if her intent was to say my client is a "narcissist," I want to nudge her to expand, elaborate, and ideally fabricate new stories on the fly about his "involvement with the mafia" or "hidden cash under the floorboards" or "habitual drug use" or "[insert something else bathshit-crazy here]." The same is true for my female clients and their ex-husbands. I want to make the opposition slippery-slope-slip into pure irrationality before the judge in order to smoke their case.

Here's why—and how.

Meet Raymond, the Smoker

Raymond was a client on our consulting side. He'd been put through the ringer of a highly expensive, highly combative divorce case. A successful and somewhat eccentric man, Raymond was used to saying things off the cuff, using his chosen bold communication style as a filter for customers he wished to work with in his business—and to filter out those he did not. In other words, Raymond would say some nutty things and swear frequently. Not an ideal starting point for court.

Over the months preceding the divorce trial, we worked with Raymond to better control his communication patterns, specifically on setting up frames of argument and storytelling for the purposes of his eventual testimony in court.

We also put Raymond through our own mock cross-examinations to give him a feel of how quickly emotional states can change under duress. Now, here is where the real lessons came.

Raymond's Direct Examination

We instructed Raymond to cover and discuss as many of the more "ludicrous" claims made by his ex-wife under his own direct examination and reframe these claims as either purposeful manipulation *by* his ex-wife or as unfortunate statements she had made resulting from her own mental health struggles.

Raymond described the impact these claims had on his life, recounting the hurtful effects they had on him as well as his relationship with her. Raymond talked about his experience with therapy to help manage and cope with the pain of these allegations (true) and found new inspiration for personal growth in spite of the claims being false and malicious. In the end, he said he was a better man for meeting his wife—and said thank you.

Raymond's Cross-Examination

Raymond's credible, measured, sympathetic tone throughout direct examination provided considerable defensive posturing when cross-examination came. From an outsider's perspective, Raymond had appeared to open his heart and mind in direct examination and gave an earnest recollection of events as he remembered them. There were mistakes he made during the marriage; these were acknowledged and accepted. This makes the cross-examiner's role of "bad guy" much more challenging, as coming in *hot* and throwing as much at the wall to see what sticks just looks bad, i.e., unprofessional and unethical. Judges don't like this.

Raymond had a great cross-examination experience, remained calm, and mostly recounted what was already said during the direct examination.

Meet Stephanie, Raymond's Ex-Wife, the Smoked

Stephanie spent hours sitting, watching, stewing in what she perceived as Raymond's "lies" during direct and cross-examination. Stephanie, for lack of a better word, was *furious*. You could almost see the smoke billowing from her eyes bordering her rage-red cheeks.

Stephanie's Direct Examination

So, up went Stephanie for her direct examination—which is approximately when I knew we had won the case for Raymond. Stephanie's lawyer started asking her questions about the incidents that Raymond described in his examination earlier. Stephanie began recounting her own version of events, which we knew already—that is, until she realized her version (as presented in every moment up to this point) was no longer enough. She felt compelled to go "Hyper-Emotional." And the fireworks began.

Rather than sticking to her story, Stephanie began adding to the story, piece-by-piece, twist-by-twist, each detail crazier than the next. Raymond went from a "guy with some cash sales" to "a member of organized crime." Raymond went from "a narcissist" to a "physically abusive husband." And he suddenly went from perhaps "not the nicest husband" to a "vile, shady, terribly abusive piece of shit." You get the idea.

We watched and smiled seeing Stephanie go off-book, realizing that in her hyper-emotional state, she made the catastrophic error of doubling-down and magnifying events into absurdity. There was no coming back from this.

Stephanie's Cross-Examination

When cross-examination came, what needed to be done was obvious: Start asking Hyper-Logical Questions about her Hyper-Emotional Statements, thereby permanently obliterating Stephanie's credibility. We would simply run through all these various *new* accusations and simply ask for evidence. Here's how that went:

> "You stated Raymond is a member of organized crime. Do you have any evidence to present which supports this?"

> "No, I just *know* he is. Just look at him! His favorite restaurant is Italian."

> "Does liking Italian food make you a member of organized crime?"

"No, but in this case it's because he's a member of organized crime."

"OK, thanks. You stated that Raymond was physically abusive. Do you have any evidence to present which supports this?"

"I mean . . no, but . . . he just—he just was. He totally was."

"Really? You didn't speak with anyone, take pictures, document this, text a friend about it, nothing?"

"No, I didn't. But he *did* do it."

And so on.

Stephanie made a grievous error—feeling like she was losing the case, she decided to dramatically escalate the severity of her claims, none of which had any basis in reality. And so with her credibility dismantled, the rest of the case fell into place for Raymond.

- Custody was granted for his children with parental decision-making rights.
- He paid Stephanie once-off alimony and her share of marital property, but both amounts were close to what his side had offered prior to trial (she had hoped to and assumed she would win far more at trial).
- Raymond's business valuation was ruled to be lower than it easily could have been, saving millions of dollars.

Raymond won by being a calm, credible, sympathetic, and presentable witness in an unfortunate divorce. And his ex-wife lost by presenting as a batshit-crazy woman who would say *anything* to win. Stephanie's credibility self-destruction altered the judge's perception of everything her side put forward. It was obvious she desired to skew results in her seemingly unfair favor, and so by granting Raymond relative victory in the divorce, the judge "equalized" the two parties. The law isn't fair, but it is equal.

Without credibility, there is nothing left.

Raymond's side smoked Stephanie's. She had nothing left.

CHAPTER 12

FAILURE AT THE LAST

For a slim percentage of high net worth would-be divorcees, the entire divorce process stalls at the finish line—or worse, after the finish line. Let me tell you about Schrodinger's Divorce (referring to the famous experiment performed by a fellow called Schrodinger who put a cat in a box and thus could not confirm if the cat was alive or dead so concluded the cat was *both*).

Now, Sean and Stacy had a tumultuous and messy divorce process, and I was parachuted in several years post-separation by a near-broken Sean and his frustrated legal counsel. (I received his first email asking for my help just past 3:00 a.m. early one morning, his local time. Timestamps reveal how bad a situation really is.)

Sean to that point had done everything "right." He had agreed to enter the collaborative divorce process with Stacy (her idea). He just wanted to reach an "amicable" solution with her. But it backfired; there was no kumbaya. Stacy had absolutely flipped when discovery revealed some of Sean's . . . proclivities. That took two years. And so an upset Stacy and embarrassed Sean entered mediation. That meant hello new attorneys and goodbye money, attention, time, and energy.

And so Sean and Stacy attended mediation, and Sean had to have his businesses, assets, and income valued—a second time. But mediation failed. Upset-Stacy decided that Sean's valuator was wrong, so she hired her own. Sean paid for it. For another couple years, Sean (well-demoralized by that point) was again raked over the coals by Stacy's valuator and attorney. They did eventually attend mediation again, and once again it failed. Stacy wanted more, and so Upset-Stacy became Ragey-Stacy.

You may be wondering how much all this melodrama had cost so far: more than $250,000 in professional fees and unfathomable amounts of attention, time, and energy. And then Ragey-Stacy pushed everything into litigation. Several more years flew by, with accusatory letters exchanged, threats made, children held hostage, and so on—all of which meant new boats for the attorneys, who were also frustrated. The boats made it all better (for them).

Ragey-Stacy was exacting revenge. Sean was breaking and needed help badly.

Harsh Truth, but It Pays

This is the painful fact of every high net worth divorce matter: A given divorce moves at the pace of the slower party. Always and without fail. This can be by design, of course, as a slow, tedious, costly divorce is plausibly deniable vengeance, particularly when one party feels slighted as Stacy did. To her, it was only "fair" to make Sean suffer after what he had done. Yes, this meant the children suffered, too, due to the limbo of uncertain home life for basically their entire childhood, but this I perceive was intentional—the children's suffering hurt Sean even worse. He knew it. She knew it. Everybody knew it.

That said, bleeding out the other party of any remaining morale and money is an effective way to negotiate the outcomes desired. Remember, well-played mind games leave the other player, unbeknownst to what's really going on, desperate for an end to the pain. That's just about where Sean was.

He was about to, after all these years, snatch defeat from the jaws of victory. What he needed was some composure. Boundaries. Confidence. And no more unwisely emotional letters back-and-forth. No more getting riled up. What you've learned about no-fault divorce, I relayed to Sean. I found a receptive audience. He was ready—to recognize the game being played and play it back better.

So what did we do? After years of Sean just about begging for all this to end, year after year with no resolution, we turned the tables. We made Ragey-Stacy be the one to have to start chasing. We strategically brought Sean into incognito mode and made him difficult to reach (not for the kids, of course). This took a number of weeks, but as we pulled Stacy off-balance, we restored the balance—specifically by playing several mind games from Chapter 7 that you know well enough by now that you can probably guess what they are.

Result: After twelve years, Sean and Stacy are finally divorced. The suffering is over.

But if Stacy and not Sean had hired me, it wouldn't be. There's a lesson in there.

CHAPTER 13

HOW THE RICH RESET AFTER DIVORCE

U p until this point, we've discussed everything leading up to "D-Day," the actual date a divorce is finalized. You have probably noticed that winning in this book has been implicitly (and now finally explicitly) defined as saving "MATE," that is, **Money, Attention, Time** and **Energy**. What I call the "Stay Rich Reset," which I recommend to all my high net worth clients, is all about maximizing each.

In my experience with many smart and still-rich divorcees, "rich" has as much to do with quality of life as quantity of money. Sure, assets matter, but (most often) men use money as a mere proxy for quality. It's akin to golf, where the scorecard shows you how well you played that round.

So, here's how the smart and rich play the post-divorce game of life and reset. Put differently, *this is how the rich stay rich.*

The Stay Rich Reset

The Stay Rich Reset comprises "Four Pillars." These are the four essential supports of the ultimate rich lifestyle, where men choose to invest their MATE post-marriage and so walk away from their divorce *richer* than ever before.

Understand that amid divorce, in particular men are time-stretched, as they are "doing divorce" while running their businesses and maintaining various personal relationships. Once it's all done, they have fewer pure commitments, specifically those that demand their time. Often that for men means losing time with their children, yes, but that frees up that time to invest in themselves, make noticeable and measurable improvements (gains), and then *increase* the quality of the time they do get with their children. And more than time, but money and attention and energy as well.

The First Pillar: Strength

This is the first pillar that the smart and rich invest their MATE into building during and after divorce. I mean literal, physical strength. Strength training results in mental clarity, physical fitness, and spiritual growth. The meme of the low-intelligence "gym bro" is incorrect. To build muscle is to build brain cells. A divorcee's money, attention, time, and energy are thus wisely invested *daily* in physical fitness. The individual can become the person physically and mentally their ex deeply desired but now can't have—and also now get into a relationship they have control over. That's strength.

Just don't forget the cardio.

The Second Pillar: Fortitude

This is emotional self-regulation—specifically, experiencing emotion, not acting on them, and honing communication skills so as not to make unforced errors in all areas of life.

After divorce, fortitude means being better able to handle dark feelings and better able to manage their children/relationships/business as well because they are making decisions more methodically, thinking much further out in time than what's pressing on the schedule immediately.

The Third Pillar: Great Relationships

Those who do this well, being able to self-regulate, are not bitter losers, nor "PTDD"—post-traumatic divorce disorder. In fact, they come out of divorce happier, sunnier, more optimistic about the future, and with greater abundance thinking.

The rich who divorced and stayed rich are now in the ideal position for setting boundaries, setting expectations, and setting standards in a partner (business, romantic, and otherwise). That said, one doesn't need to endure divorce to be able to do that, but *all* of these traits come from trial by fire one way or another. Any personal or business relationships, even the corporate divorce (shareholder disagreement, suing each other, for instance) and longtime friendships that failed, when analyzed, can have that pain transmuted into self-assuredness in future relationships (including instinct for which potential relationships to avoid and getting out before it's too late).

The Fourth Pillar: Capital Gains

Divorce for the smart rich means more time to devote to their operating company or to find tertiary companies to invest in or grow. And so millionaires become multimillionaires . . . multimillionaires become decamillionaires and beyond. Again, it's about the money, but it's not *all* about the money.

Because by investing their MATE to build up these Four Pillars, these wealthy individuals see incredible, worthwhile gains and live richer lives. (Notice investing versus *spending* their MATE).

I talk to my clients about the Four Pillars even prior to divorce. It's a night and day difference compared to most divorce cases. There's palpable optimism, self-assurance, good-humoredness, productivity, focus, *happiness* even—because they have something specific to do, and a reason to do it. A brighter future is ahead of them, and the worst is over. Contrast that with the newly divorced who sink into depression, whose perspective is, *The worst has just begun.*

For those who do it right—who complete the Rich Divorce Reset—the future is all possibilities. And for many men, one of those possibilities, I like to call the "green pill."

Taking the Green Pill (or Not)

The red pill is a metaphor for uncomfortable truth; the blue pill, for comfortable lies. The green pill is something else entirely but just as interesting. As I begin to explain, you'll get it right away.

During my 2023-2024 business season, I counted twenty new clients who all said almost verbatim (half of them unprompted by me) the following:

> I am never getting married again. But I have an . . . *arrangement* now.

That's how they all said it, too, with the pause then the emphasis. For many men, a reinforced-steel prenuptial agreement is acceptable for their next spouse (so long as that spouse agrees, of course). For others, there can be trust issues. And priorities. So literal pay-to-play relationships are acceptable. They are short term, both individuals get what they want from the other, and everything is bought and paid for. Usually, the green-pilled male will get a vasectomy first to prevent multi-million-dollar "baby-trapping" (which happens more often than you'd be comfortable with, if you knew exactly how often it did).

Taking the green pill post-divorce is like hiring a consultant. It's transactional. Less commitment. But dating for remarriage is like seeking a business partner or joint investor. For the latter individuals, coming to understand at great depth the **ART** of relationships is key.

Making ART Post-Divorce

ART stands for **Attraction, Respect**, and **Trust**, all of which the smart and rich seek to give out and receive back in their next meaningful, long-term relationship following the end of their previous marriage. Often, ART is done in these future relationships *because* it did not exist in their prior relationship. Never again will they pull a, as was probably the case, "You stay home with the kids and I'll go out and be famous and make all the money." This time, they know what they want. And what they want to give. Communication, boundaries, and confidence to communicate the boundaries!

And adventure. So key. Smart, rich divorcees make efforts to include their new partner, going out of their way to include in the adventure so they are in it together, feeling like a team, with mutual support—a positive feedback loop of experiences. The more ART that gets made in a relationship, the better it gets, and the easier it gets to put in even more, and so on.

As an aside, most marriages ultimately break down due to trust, and it starts with getting caught in a lie—usually it's the guy's fault (sorry, harsh truth). Something happened that shouldn't have happened, *but he lied about it.* "The cover-up is worse than the crime."

Those who give and receive trust are open, authentic. *This is who I am. I will not capitulate my values. I will not act differently to make you accept me or to try to make sure this relationship works*, essentially. By the way, that's what they did in their first marriage, most likely. It's harder to reestablish boundaries to where you want them than it is to build them where they need to be in the first place.

And so the rich protect themselves before, during, and after divorce, and that's how they stay rich. To protect yourself is not to be guarded, but to be open. Your shield is yourself. These successful divorcees become themselves again. They didn't know who they were when they first got married though, so it's rediscovering what they did not discover in the first place. Finding what they looked for, finally. It's good to be rich and divorced.

But there's one more thing.

What if all this information was good and helpful, yes, but there remains another possibility? A possibility that there will not, in fact, even BE a divorce?

What if you or your client don't have to endure the end of marriage in order to live a rich life?

What if indeed.

That's a valid consideration many of you have at this precise point in the book. And so while this book may be drawing to a close, the chapters are not.

To get the free bonus chapter—Chapter 14 What If?—go to www.stayrichdivorce.com/bonus. Because there very well may be a way to stay rich *and* stay married, and be better for having done so. It will take the most counterintuitive advice on the matter, however, and I must forewarn you—the material in Chapter 14 may make most of you *very* uncomfortable. You may even ask for a refund on this book *and* leave it a one-star review after you read the bonus chapter.

Let's see what happens. **Go to www.stayrichdivorce.com/bonus to get your free bonus chapter: Chapter 14 What If?**

ACKNOWLEDGMENTS

To My Family, Who Support.
To My Children, Who Inspire.
To The Love of My Life, Who I Admire.
To My Mentors, Who Guided Me Here.
To My Editor, Joshua Lisec, Who Made This Book Shine.
To My Clients, Who Invite Me Into Their Lives.
Thank You.
This Is All For You.

ABOUT THE AUTHOR

Ryan Bensen, MBA, CPA, CA, CBV, ABV, CFE, CFF is an expert witness and litigation consultant for high net worth and ultra high net worth divorce cases. Since 2011, Ryan has worked with courts to determine appropriate business valuations and with clients to achieve overwhelmingly favorable outcomes. He has uncovered in excess of $250 million in hidden assets and turned many ex-wives into multi-million-aires. Learn more about Ryan's work at www.stayrichdivorce.com.